OECD ECONOMIC SURVEYS

1999-2000

SPAIN

ORGANISATION FOR ECONOMIC CO-OPERATION AND DEVELOPMENT

ORGANISATION FOR ECONOMIC CO-OPERATION AND DEVELOPMENT

Pursuant to Article 1 of the Convention signed in Paris on 14th December 1960, and which came into force on 30th September 1961, the Organisation for Economic Co-operation and Development (OECD) shall promote policies designed:

- to achieve the highest sustainable economic growth and employment and a rising standard of living in Member countries, while maintaining financial stability, and thus to contribute to the development of the world economy;
- to contribute to sound economic expansion in Member as well as non-member countries in the process of economic development; and
- to contribute to the expansion of world trade on a multilateral, non-discriminatory basis in accordance with international obligations.

The original Member countries of the OECD are Austria, Belgium, Canada, Denmark, France, Germany, Greece, Iceland, Ireland, Italy, Luxembourg, the Netherlands, Norway, Portugal, Spain, Sweden, Switzerland, Turkey, the United Kingdom and the United States. The following countries became Members subsequently through accession at the dates indicated hereafter: Japan (28th April 1964), Finland (28th January 1969), Australia (7th June 1971), New Zealand (29th May 1973), Mexico (18th May 1994), the Czech Republic (21st December 1995), Hungary (7th May 1996), Poland (22nd November 1996) and Korea (12th December 1996). The Commission of the European Communities takes part in the work of the OECD (Article 13 of the OECD Convention).

Publié également en français.

Table of contents

BASIC STATISTICS OF SPAIN (1998)

THE LAND

Area (sq. km)	505 990	Major cities, 1996 (thousand inhabitants)	
Cultivated area (sq. km)	187 530	Madrid	2 867
		Barcelona	1 509
		Valencia	747
		Seville	697
		Saragossa	602

THE PEOPLE

Population (thousands), 1997	39 323	Civilian employment (thousands):	13 205
Number of inhabitants per sq. km, 1997	77.7	by sector (per cent of total):	
Net natural increase (thousands), 1997	2	Agriculture	8.0
Net migration (thousands), 1996	47	Industry	20.5
		Construction	9.9
		Services	61.6

PRODUCTION

Gross domestic product, GDP		GDP at factor cost by origin	
(billion pesetas)	86 964	(per cent of total):	
GDP per head (US$)	14 676	Agriculture	4.4
Gross fixed investment		Industry	23.1
Per cent of GDP	22.7	Construction	7.6
Per head (US$)	3 327	Services	64.9

THE GOVERNMENT

Public consumption (per cent of GDP)	17.4	Composition of Parliament	
Fixed investment (per cent of gross fixed		(number of seats):	350
capital formation)	13.6	Popular Party (PP)	156
Government revenue (per cent of GDP)	37.1	Spanish Labour Socialist Party (PSOE)	141
General government deficit		Izquierda Unida	21
(per cent of GDP)	2.3	Convergence and Union (CIU)	16
		Basque Nationalist Party (PNV)	5
		Canarian Union (CC)	4
		Herri Batasuna	2
		Other	5

Last general elections: March 1996

FOREIGN TRADE

Exports of goods and services:		Imports of goods and services:	
(billion US$)	158.0	(billion US$)	156.1
(per cent of GDP)	27.1	(per cent of GDP)	26.8
Exports as a per cent of total merchandise		Imports as a per cent of total merchandise	
exports, customs basis:		imports, customs basis:	
Foodstuffs	12.6	Foodstuffs	7.0
Other consumer goods	28.2	Other consumer goods	19.0
Energy	2.0	Energy	6.4
Other intermediate goods	42.8	Other intermediate goods	50.1
Capital goods	14.3	Capital goods	17.4

THE CURRENCY

Monetary unit: Peseta		Currency units per US$, average	
		of daily figures:	
		Year 1998	149.4
		November 1999	161.1

Note: An international comparison of certain basic statistics is given in an Annex table.

This Survey is based on the Secretariat's study prepared for the annual review of Spain by the Economic and Development Review Committee on 25th November 1999.

•

After revisions in the light of discussions during the review, final approval of the Survey for publication was given by the Committee on 10th December 1999.

•

The previous Survey of Spain was issued in March 1998.

Assessment and recommendations

Spain's economic performance has been impressive...

Spain is enjoying the third year of strong growth. Sound macroeconomic management, including fiscal consolidation, laid the foundation for entry to the European Monetary Union at the beginning of 1999. Interest rates eased considerably prior to entry, boosting economic activity in 1998 and 1999, while moderate wage claims and progress in reforming the labour market have bolstered job creation. Inflation has slowed to historically low levels, though it has remained above the euro area average. The good performance has also been underpinned by important progress in critical areas of structural reform. Product market competition has been enhanced and the functioning of capital markets has improved, while the privatisation process, one of the most ambitious in the OECD, has been further stepped up. Moreover, the 1999 personal income tax reform has redressed distortions and improved tax neutrality. As a result of sustained growth, Spain's per capita GDP has come closer to the EU average. However, despite a sharp decline, the unemployment rate still remains the highest in the OECD.

... but policies need to be geared to sustaining the favourable growth prospects

The economy showed remarkable resilience in the wake of the slow-down prompted by the emerging economies' crisis. As discussed in Chapter I of the Survey, which reviews macroeconomic developments, activity is projected to remain robust, with growth outpacing the OECD average over the next two years. The main risk to the outlook stems from underlying domestic demand pressures, which may induce costs rising faster than in the euro area, thus undermining competitiveness and threatening the sustainability of employment growth. By offsetting the impact of easy monetary conditions, a tighter fiscal policy stance would address overheating risks and secure the favourable growth prospects of the economy. Chapter II reviews structural policy initiatives, in the light of the government's commitment to modernise the economy, so as to converge rapidly with higher-income countries. Major challenges ahead include keeping up the pace of labour market reform and further enhancing product market competition to promote strong non-inflationary growth. Far-reaching reforms will also be needed to secure the sustainability of the pension system in the medium term. Chapter III discusses the strengths and weaknesses of the Spanish tax system, reviews recent tax reform initiatives, and discusses policy options to streamline the tax system further, promote tax neutrality and enhance tax decentralisation.

Domestic demand and employment have continued to grow briskly...

Domestic demand, which rose by 5 per cent in both 1998 and 1999, continued to be the driving force of economic growth. Household demand accelerated further in 1999, spurred by the cut in personal income taxes, low interest rates and strong consumer confidence. This cushioned the slight deceleration in business investment due to the weaker international environment. Owing to the stronger upturn in Spain than in the EU as a whole, net exports became an increasing drag on growth. As a result, output growth slowed slightly, from 4 per cent in 1998 to perhaps 3¾ per cent in 1999, which is nevertheless still far above the OECD average. Reflecting strong activity, moderate wage claims and cuts in non-wage labour costs, the unemployment rate has fallen from 22 per cent in 1996 to 15 per cent by the end of 1999 and is projected to decline further. On the other hand, productivity growth slowed sharply, which may in part reflect measurement problems, though it may also partly reflect other factors, for instance, the low productivity of a large number of jobs created in the service and construction sectors, or the lower-than-average skills of workers recently drawn into employment.

... and disinflation has stalled

The headline inflation rate edged up during 1999, to 2.7 per cent in November 1999 from 1.4 per cent in December 1998. This largely reflects the hike in oil and food prices, with the underlying rate of inflation remaining around 2¼ per cent since 1998. However, though inflation for traded goods has remained subdued, buoyant demand combined with weak competition in some service sectors has pushed up profit margins, and the inflation differential with the euro area average has consequently widened. In the construction sector, the boom in demand has been reflected in a rise in housing prices of 9 per cent over the last year, while the wage drift has been strong. Demand pressures have also been reflected in a worsening of the current account, which has turned to deficit since 1998. The deficit could reach 1 per cent of GDP in 1999 and is projected to widen further.

Monetary conditions have eased, while the pace of fiscal consolidation has slowed

Monetary conditions have become gradually easier since late 1995 and were eased further as the European Central Bank reduced interest rates in April 1999, and as the euro depreciated. With inflation rising faster than in the euro area since 1998, real interest rates have fallen further below the euro area average. As from 1998 the pace of fiscal consolidation has slowed compared with the strong adjustment effort in 1996 and 1997, prior to EMU membership. A major personal income tax reform was implemented by the 1999 budget. Even so, the 1999 budget deficit is officially projected to drop to 1.3 per cent of GDP, from 2.3 per cent in 1998, thanks to stronger-than-expected indirect and corporate tax collections and to a surge in social security revenues underpinned by the booming labour market. The 2000 budget aims at further reducing the general government's deficit to 0.8 per cent of GDP. This would mostly come from lower debt service payments and cyclical factors, as the budget also plans to increase social spending, step up infrastructure investment and increase corporate tax breaks for R&D expenses, while excise taxes are to be frozen to help achieve the 1999 inflation target. The impact of these measures on the structural deficit will probably be only partly offset by maintaining the hiring restrictions for civil servants and restraining subsidies to public enterprises.

Activity should remain strong and cost pressures may threaten competitiveness

While domestic demand growth is projected to edge down, as the stimulus to consumption from the personal income tax cut wanes and monetary conditions in the euro area are projected to tighten a bit, exports should gradually rebound as a result of the improved international environment. Overall, growth will remain above potential. Past favourable cost developments, which in recent years have mitigated the effect on prices of fairly high growth in unit labour costs, are likely to be reversed. Aside from the uncertain prospects for oil and primary commodity prices, the scope for a further decline in firms' financial and non-wage labour costs is low. Furthermore, the higher headline inflation rate in recent months could raise wages, as a large share of wage settlements contains an indexation clause. Additionally, the progressive tightening of the labour market is likely to heighten wage claims. Adverse domestic cost developments may weaken competitiveness and be reflected in an even sharper widening of the current account deficit. The deficit is already projected to increase to 3 per cent of GDP by 2001.

A tighter fiscal policy stance would reduce overheating risks

With the loss of the exchange rate instrument to offset changes in relative costs, faltering competitiveness could threaten the sustainability of recent strong employment and output growth. Despite some projected tightening in the two years ahead, the stance of monetary policy in the euro area may not be in tune with the more advanced cyclical position of the Spanish economy. A tighter fiscal stance than embodied in the authorities' current targets would be appropriate to rebalance the policy mix and reduce the risk of overheating. In addition, moderate wage agreements would ensure that labour cost developments are kept in line with the euro area, thus safeguarding competitiveness.

More ambitious public expenditure restraint would provide increased scope to deal with upcoming policy challenges

Spain's Stability Programme targets a declining deficit, turning to a slight surplus of 0.1 per cent of GDP by 2002, with the projected debt-to-GDP ratio falling below 60 per cent. On current spending and entitlement programmes, some medium-term savings could be expected from further cuts in the wage bill due to the restrictions on hiring civil servants; downsizing of transfers to utilities still in public hands; lower outlays for unemployment benefits as the slack in the labour market recedes; and better management of health services thanks to recent reforms. Nevertheless, medium-term pressures on the budget could offset the projected savings, owing to increased public investment outlays to upgrade core infrastructure, as well as higher pension liabilities and health care costs due to population ageing. To accommodate these pressures, at least partly, and to further reduce the tax wedge on labour, more ambitious spending cuts will be needed. Stronger spending cuts would also provide more room for fiscal manoeuvre, while complying with the EU's Stability and Growth Pact.

Population ageing requires an overhaul of the pension system

Reflecting the recent boom in employment and the specifics of the age pyramid, the pay-as-you-go pension system will be broadly balanced in 1999 and for some years ahead. However, its continued maturation and inherent generosity will add to future budgetary pressures. In view of the prospective rise in the old-age dependency ratio, pension benefits are generous, both relative to contributions and by international standards. Specifically, the replacement rate is high, the pensions' base narrow and the accumulation pattern of pension rights front-loaded. As a result, the future unfunded liabilities of the pension system are sizeable. The creation of a reserve fund in 2000 is a step to attenuate the severity of reforms that will have to occur at a later date. However, to secure the viability of the pension system, the renegotiation of the Toledo Pact in 2000 should consider reducing the generosity of the system, as increases in contributions could harm employment. Specifically, this would entail broadening the pension base and tightening eligibility conditions. Of particular concern in a tightening labour market are the strong incentives to retire early. In this regard, a key measure would consist of further reducing the rate at which pension rights are accumulated, while increases in minimum non-contributory pensions should be avoided as they risk reinforcing incentives to retire early. Complementing the pay-as-you-go system with a funded pension system should also be encouraged by setting up a regulatory framework for company-based and individual complementary pension schemes.

The 1997 labour market reform has supported job creation...

The 1997 labour market reform has reduced the high level of employment protection legislation. The introduction of a new permanent job contract with reduced severance payments and lower social security contributions has supported the remarkable labour market performance and improved employment prospects for the targeted groups, especially the young. Nevertheless, fixed-term employment has remained widespread, while the co-existence of many different types of contracts with different incentives is of concern, as it tends to perpetuate labour market segmentation and might entail displacement effects. More comprehensive steps to ease employment protection legislation, encompassing core worker groups, would help sustain the current surge in employment growth and improve the allocation of human resources. Enhancing the effectiveness of active labour market policies is also needed to improve employment prospects of workers with difficulties to enter the labour market. Other measures introduced by the 1997 reform were less effective. In particular, existing legislation on unfair dismissals should be clarified to ensure that the decisions of labour courts, which rule on severance payments in most individual dismissal cases, conform to its spirit. Moreover, the wage bargaining system has remained fairly rigid. It should be reformed to enhance companies' flexibility and take better account of differences in the slack in regional labour markets.

... but more comprehensive initiatives are needed to reduce structural unemployment further

Looking forward, further labour market reforms will be needed to reduce the structural rate of unemployment and consolidate the strong growth of employment without creating bottlenecks. Because labour market institutions interact with policies in other areas, reforms should be comprehensive. Policy measures would thus be mutually reinforcing and have a wider impact. Policy should address in particular the low geographic mobility of labour, which increases structural unemployment and perpetuates large unemployment discrepancies across regions. To foster labour mobility, policy should aim at enhancing the development of the market for rental housing. This would require easing restrictive regulations on the length of rental contracts, liberalising urban land supply – to slow the surge in home prices and rentals – and lowering the still very generous tax preferences to owner-occupied housing. Restricting the very loose eligibility conditions for income support for seasonally unemployed farm workers should also strengthen labour mobility. To enhance active job search, compensating the unemployed for the job loss should take into account severance payments, which are high and under specific circumstances tax-exempt. To further promote labour market flexibility, the new part-time work regulation should be softened.

Promoting competition in product markets would boost potential output

Regulatory reforms, in particular in the telecommunications sector, have demonstrated that competition can stimulate service improvements and induce price declines at the same time. Further progress along these lines would boost potential output, reduce cost pressures and enhance competitiveness. The energy sector has been granted priority in this respect since it provides critical inputs for the rest of the economy. In the oil distribution sector, recent measures to raise price transparency and to streamline abstruse licensing regulations are a step in the right direction. However, restrictive regulations governing the supply of land by local authorities could still limit the opening of new petrol stations and thus inhibit competition. In the electricity sector, despite rapid and broad deregulation efforts, the market is still highly concentrated, and prices before tax are still among the highest in the OECD. Reaping the full benefits of the deregulation process would require fostering competition in electricity generation. Liberalisation of the gas market should be accelerated. Moreover, more flexible shopping hours would benefit consumers and create new employment opportunities. Public support programmes to industry have also increased rapidly in recent years. To minimise possible distortions to competition, support to industry – especially that delivered under regional development and technology-specific R&D programmes – should have a clear focus on horizontal objectives.

Granting sufficient powers and resources to independent regulatory and competition bodies is needed

Transferring powers to independent regulators (sector-specific as well as a general competition watch-dog), and ensuring that their financial and staff resources are sufficient, is the key to promoting a competition-friendly environment. The government intends to reform the 1989 competition law to raise the effectiveness of the existing competition bodies. Transferring powers to independent sector-specific bodies, rather than giving them merely advisory roles, should also be considered. In particular, the legal authority of the Energy Commission, which will supersede the Electricity Commission in 2000, should

be enhanced. This would boost confidence in the independence of energy-related decisions, thus encouraging entry
into the sectors. In the telecommunications sector, the divi-
sion of responsibility between the Ministry of Development
and the sectoral regulator (*Comision del Mercado de Telecomunicaciones*) should be clarified. In particular, if price regulation
for the incumbent is deemed necessary, it should be transferred from the government to the independent sectoral
body.

*Despite improved
regulation,
support to public
services remains
sizeable and
needs downsizing*

The still sizeable support to public utilities burdens the
budget. Though the public service character of rail and
urban transport – as well as the resulting positive externalities – may warrant a certain degree of subsidisation, revenues should be enhanced and operating costs reduced. The
ongoing programme of rail infrastructure modernisation
could, in the long run, restore the attractiveness of rail
transport. Nevertheless, to reduce costs in the short run,
steps should be taken to rationalise the network, possibly
by franchising parts of rail operations. In the postal services,
recent steps to upgrade the regulatory framework have
enhanced transparency and part of the market has been
liberalised, while basic nation-wide services at affordable
prices were guaranteed. The debt of the public broadcasting corporation has been soaring. If maintaining the public
service in broadcasting is deemed necessary, revenue
enhancing through user fees should be considered.

*The regulatory
framework has
changed in the
right direction,
but the
performance of
the financial
sector can be
strengthened*

Banking consolidation has gained momentum, partly
spurred by the prospect of the development of a more
integrated banking industry in the euro area. Thanks to an
active policy of mergers and acquisitions, Spanish banks
have acquired strategic stakes with a particular focus on the
Latin America market. Further progress in rationalising the
banking system should reduce excess capacity and high
operating costs – which reflect the branch-intensive character of Spanish banking – and reap greater efficiency gains. It
would be advisable to promote ownership forms of savings
banks that would make them more sensitive to market
forces. Vigilance on the part of the supervisory authorities
should continue as declining profitability may induce banks
to take more risks in lending and asset management

– though high capitalisation of Spanish banks provides a cushion for higher exposure to risks, especially in Latin America. Asset price inflation in the housing market needs to be monitored, with a view to raising bank lending standards should collateral prices become inflated, so as to limit risks of an unsustainable credit expansion. Capital market deepening has been supported by deregulation and massive privatisations, though the structure of the market remains relatively unbalanced, with the low level of private bond issuance signalling a still difficult access of private businesses to non-bank financing. Overall, the regulatory framework has changed in the right direction and the need for further reform – especially to enhance SMEs access to the capital markets – should be assessed in the light of the business response to the newly created opportunities.

The tax system needs to be simplified to improve enforcement, while broadening the tax base would allow tax rates to be reduced further

The 1998 personal income tax reform embodied an important simplification effort, but further steps in this direction are required. The Spanish tax system is still characterised by a large number of tax reliefs and special regimes. As a result, tax expenditures are high and, despite rather high statutory rates, the productivity of the tax system is low by international standards. Some preferential tax schemes have been implemented to mitigate structural rigidities of the Spanish economy. However, tackling these rigidities through broad-ranging structural reforms could prove to be more cost-effective. This would involve, for instance, easing the regulatory constraints on the supply of land while scaling back the remaining tax incentives for owner-occupied housing. Streamlining the tax system would, in turn, facilitate enforcement and reduce compliance costs. For instance, the "forfaitaire" system of taxation ("módulos") for unincorporated business and the self-employed is still complex, and should be replaced by proper accounting rules. Broadening the personal income tax base by further streamlining tax expenditures and reviewing existing special tax regimes would allow a further reduction of tax rates and thus enhance incentives to work, invest and save.

Reducing the tax wedge on labour would support job creation

Though the tax wedge on labour income is not very high by European standards and has been reduced in recent years, a number of rigidities in labour and product markets may have facilitated forward shifting of taxation into labour costs, thus hampering job creation. In addition, the still existing social security contribution ceilings create a regressive pattern of labour income taxation. Low-skilled workers, who often hold fixed-term jobs, may suffer more from the higher tax wedge, as wage negotiation practices and strict employment protection legislation make wage settlements reflect conditions of the well-protected segment of the labour market, rather than overall labour market slack. Moreover, social security floors may discourage lower-qualified persons from entering the formal labour market, thus promoting employment in the underground economy. Suppressing the minimum social security payments and further cutting social security contribution rates at the low end of the income scale is thus of immediate concern. In this regard, as a first best, lower expenditure could finance revenue shortfalls. As a second best, social security contribution ceilings could be lifted more rapidly. Shifting the tax mix onto other tax bases could also be considered. The upcoming reform of social security in the context of the *Toledo Pact* could provide an opportunity to reduce non-wage labour costs significantly.

Promoting tax neutrality across saving instruments and better focusing tax incentives to investment would enhance efficiency

By international comparison, the tax system in Spain is fairly neutral across capital assets and sources of investment financing, while progress towards greater tax neutrality across saving instruments has been a hallmark of the 1998 personal income tax reform. However, the tax system still encourages investment in housing and favours long holding periods, especially for investment in life insurance and pension schemes. In addition, the taxation of dividends through the personal income tax gives firms an incentive to retain their earnings, while providing shareholders with more lightly taxed capital gains. Further strengthening tax neutrality would enhance financial market liquidity, facilitate the reallocation of funds from mature, slow growing companies to more innovative firms, and promote direct share ownership. Also, the corporate income tax includes non-neutralities that should be addressed. Progressivity in the corporate rate could lead to under-invoicing in order to be eligible for the lower rates and may also distort firms' incentives to expand. Investment in R&D is granted very generous tax incentives compared to those for firm training.

Tax incentives provided by some special corporate tax regimes, as the one in the Basque Country, which vary with the amount of investment, are discriminatory and may distort competition against smaller companies that are not eligible for such aids. In addition, they may induce shifts in plant location, which are questionable on efficiency grounds. On the other hand, adopting more liberal provisions for carrying forward and backward losses in the general corporate tax regime would enhance incentives for risk taking and investment.

Granting territorial governments more revenue raising powers should go along with enhanced fiscal discipline

The 1997-2001 financing system for the regions has been an important step towards better matching spending responsibilities and revenue raising powers of the regions. However, the regions' tax base remains too narrow compared with their spending competencies and, reflecting the heavy reliance on personal income tax receipts, too volatile. The guarantee scheme, which protects the regions against temporary revenue shortfalls, has been amended in 1998 and may now fail to provide regional governments with the right incentives to pursue fiscal consolidation. Tax sharing should rely on a wider array of taxes – especially on taxes that have the advantage of generating less volatile revenues than income taxes. Greater reliance on fees-for-services should also be sought, both at the regional and local levels, to ensure a better balance between the costs and benefits of publicly provided goods. Monitoring and accountability should be enhanced by the timely publication of the regions' fiscal accounts, while the fiscal programmes agreed upon with the regional governments should be made public. Moreover, transparency concerning the financial relationship between local public enterprises and regional governments should be enhanced. Existing borrowing constraints on the regions should be made binding, while an improved mechanism for the enforcement of fiscal discipline should be sought.

Summing-up

Spain's recent economic performance has been impressive, thanks to the sharp decline in interest rates prior to joining the European Monetary Union, to sound fiscal policy and to wide-ranging structural reforms. Recent initiatives have enhanced product market competition, improved the functioning of capital markets, stepped up the privatisation process, and addressed some of the rigidities in the labour market. In addition, the tax reforms implemented since 1996 have achieved progress in streamlining the tax system and redressing distortions. To secure the favourable growth prospects of the economy, the risks stemming from strong demand pressures and unfavourable cost developments that may impair competitiveness need to be addressed by a tighter fiscal stance. Moreover, to reap the full growth dividend of past reform efforts and step up convergence with higher-income OECD economies, policy should aim at removing obstacles to non-inflationary growth through a comprehensive approach that keeps up the pace of labour market reform and further improves product market competition. Labour market reforms will need to address the full range of labour market rigidities that interact with distortions in other areas. Further progress can also be made by alleviating the tax pressure on labour income, improving neutrality in the taxation of savings and better focusing corporate tax incentives. Moreover, addressing structural weaknesses in tax decentralisation would improve efficiency and enhance fiscal discipline. To take advantage of policy complementarities, further reform of the tax system would need to proceed in tandem with labour market and social security reforms. Advancing in these ways would help both to deal with the continuing unemployment problem and to sustain the impressive economic performance over the medium term.

I.   Macroeconomic conditions

Recent macroeconomic developments

In 1999, growth has remained buoyant, with the economy showing remarkable resilience in the wake of the slow-down prompted by the emerging economies' crisis. Growth picked up to 4 per cent in 1998 and slowed only moderately to an estimated 3.7 per cent in 1999, which is still considerably above the OECD average. Output growth has been underpinned by strong domestic demand, expanding by nearly 5 per cent since 1998 – a rate not seen since the expansion in the late 1980s. Easy monetary conditions and healthy growth in households' disposable income, due to income tax cuts and rapid job creation have spurred domestic demand. The unemployment rate fell swiftly from 22 per cent in 1996 to close to 15 per cent at the end of 1999, accounting for more than 40 per cent of the decline in EU-wide unemployment. Wage inflation has remained tame so far, but due to strong domestic demand, price pressures in sheltered sectors, the rise in the oil price and the effects of the severe drought, disinflation has stalled. The underlying rate of inflation has hovered around 2¼ per cent since 1998, while Spain's inflation differential with the euro area has been widening.

Sound macroeconomic management underpinned this fine economic performance. Strong fiscal consolidation in 1996 and 1997 made Spain's commitment to becoming a founding member of the European monetary union credible, inducing a sharp decline in interest rates and laying the ground for the 1999 personal income tax reform. Monetary conditions have become exceptionally easy, especially after the European Central Bank reduced interest rates in April 1999 in a move to address concerns about deflationary tendencies in the euro area. With inflation rising faster than in the euro area, monetary conditions have become even easier in Spain, as indicated by lower-than-average real interest rates. At the same time, the pace of fiscal consolidation has slowed as from 1998, compared with the previous two years' strong adjustment efforts. The relaxed macroeconomic policy stance may make it difficult to forestall demand pressures. Domestic demand is projected to slow only slightly in the coming years, while growth will remain above potential, fuelling pressures on costs and prices. The main risk to the favourable growth outlook may thus stem from adverse domestic cost developments, as they may weaken competitiveness, widen the current account deficit, and threaten the sustainability of recent employment and output growth. To help rebalance the policy mix, fiscal policy should aim at more ambitious short-run consolidation targets. This would keep demand pressures in check and ensure that the economy remains on a path of sustained high growth.

Household demand has gathered steam

Household demand has continued to gather steam and attained its highest growth rate since the early 1990s. Housing investment and purchases of durable goods have been the most dynamic components, partly reflecting pent-up demand accumulated over several years. Car registrations have risen by two digit growth rates since 1997, thundering ahead by 21 per cent over the first 10 months of 1999, and spending on household appliances has boomed. Housing investment has also increased steeply. The rise in building permits issued approached 30 per cent in 1998 and the first half of 1999. The boom in household demand has been fuelled by the strong rise in household real disposable income, which accelerated in 1999 as sweeping personal income tax cuts added to the exceptional buoyancy of employment. The "feel-good" factor has also contributed to propel household consumption: the drop in the unemployment rate – with a large share of the newly employed under permanent contracts – prompted a slight decline in the household saving ratio in 1998 and 1999 (Figure 1, panel A). Easier financial conditions have also played a supporting role. The gradual loosening of monetary conditions, combined with fierce competition between financial institutions (see Chapter II), brought real interest rates to historically low levels. This has been accompanied by a surge in consumer and mortgage credit, which has grown by over 15 per cent since the second half of 1997 (Figure 1, panel B). The income effect of the decline in interest rates has been mitigated by the reallocation of households' portfolio from bank deposits to equity and mutual funds. Despite the sharp rise in liabilities, households' net financial wealth continued to increase, reaching 87 per cent of GDP in 1998. Moreover, real estate assets, which represent households' largest source of wealth, gained strongly in value, though less than in other European countries which have enjoyed robust growth for some years (e.g. Ireland, Finland and the Netherlands). In Spain, real estate prices rose by 13 per cent in the 18 months to the second quarter of 1999 (Table 1).

Business investment growth has remained brisk

Investment has accelerated and remains the most dynamic component of domestic demand despite the sharp slide in business sentiment in late 1998 and early 1999 in the wake of the emerging economies' crisis. Limited spare capacity and solid order books have underpinned an acceleration in business investment

Figure 1. **Household demand, saving ratio and monetary conditions**

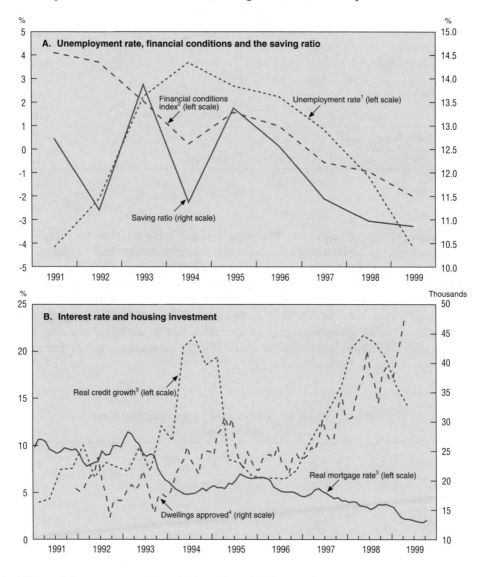

1. Difference to the average unemployment rate over the period (20 per cent).
2. The financial conditions indicator is computed as the weighted average of the real short term and long term interest rates and the real effective exchange rate (based on unit labour costs in manufacturing). The interest rate variable has a unitary coefficient while the coefficient of the exchange rate variable is the ratio of exports to GDP.
3. Deflated by the CPI.
4. 3-months moving average.
Source: OECD Secretariat and OECD, *Main Economic Indicators.*

Table 1. **Assets prices in selected OECD countries**

Increase between end 1997 and June 1999, in per cent

	Bank lending to households	Share prices	House prices
Finland	15	121	14
France	10	51	8[1]
Ireland	45[2]	27	39
Netherlands	17	28	28
Portugal	54	20	..
Spain	**32**	**45**	**13**

1. Secondary market in Paris.
2. Total private sector.
Source: OECD, *Main Economic Indicators* and National Central Banks.

in machinery and equipment. Business surveys indicate that investment has remained mainly geared towards enlarging capacity rather than substituting for labour, but recently has been adjusted towards reaping efficiency gains. The surge in business investment has been supported by historically low borrowing costs and corporate indebtedness while corporate profitability has improved, largely reflecting a further decline in financial costs and moderate wage claims (Table 2).[1] Overall, gross fixed capital formation has grown by 40 per cent in real terms from its trough in 1993. As a share of GDP, it represented 24 per cent in

Table 2. **Financial performance of non-financial firms**[1]

In per cent over previous year

	1995[2]	1996[2]	1997[2]	1998[2]	1998 Q3[3]/ 1997 Q3	1999 Q3[3]/ 1998 Q3
Gross value added	8.1	2.5	7.0	6.7	5.5	2.5
Employment	0.9	1.0	1.6	3.0	0.6	−0.6
Labour costs per employee	n.a.	3.2	2.0	1.9	3.2	1.3
Financial costs	−0.6	−13.0	−13.7	−8.7	−8.3	−7.6
Memorandum items:						
Net income[4]	7.4	11.0	15.8	19.1	20.0	24.7
Debt ratio[4]	45.7	42.4	40.7	39.6	37.6	36.8
Leverage ratio[5]	−1.0	0.5	3.8	2.7	2.5	4.5

1. Data coverage is biased towards large, public and industrial enterprises.
2. Annual sample.
3. Quarterly sample.
4. As a percentage of gross value added.
5. Rate of return of assets less financial costs on total liabilities (in percentage points).
Source: Bank of Spain, *Central de balances.*

Figure 2. **Investment in selected OECD countries**[1]

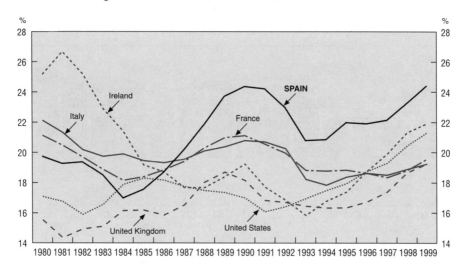

1. Ratio of investment to gross domestic product at constant prices.
Source: OECD Secretariat.

1999, far above the share observed in most other OECD countries (Figure 2). Rapid growth in the capital stock has spurred the economy's potential to grow but has also been reflected in a deterioration of the current account. Increased public and enterprise saving in the past few years has only partly offset the decline in household saving. As a result, a rising part of investment is being financed by foreign capital.

Net exports and, to a lesser extent, public consumption have acted as a drag on growth

While most private demand components gained momentum, public sector demand has remained subdued and slightly receded as a share of GDP over the past two years. This is largely due to the strict replacement rule for civil servants. In sharp contrast, public investment accelerated briskly in 1998, after several years of cutbacks, and has again risen strongly in 1999. Overall, growth of total domestic demand reached 5 per cent in 1998 and 1999, the highest rate since the end of the 1980s. Due to the relatively stronger business cycle position with respect to most other EU economies, net exports have deteriorated significantly (Figure 3). As a result, the pace of output growth is estimated to have eased slightly to around 3¾ per cent in 1999, from 4 per cent in 1998.

Figure 3. **Contributions to GDP growth**

Change over same quarter of previous year

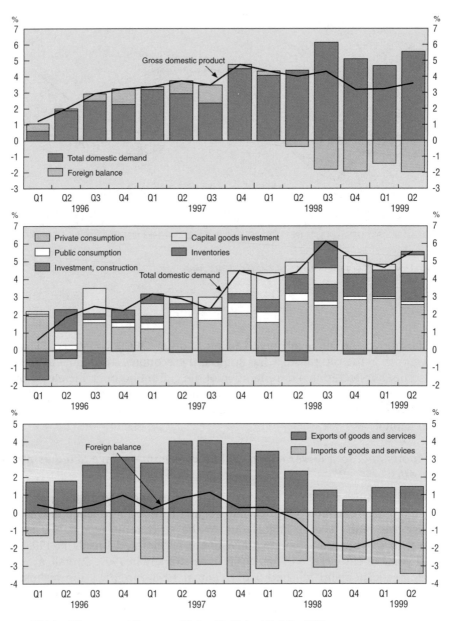

Source: Ministry of Economy and Finance and National Institute of Statistics (INE).

Employment creation has been buoyant

The employment elasticity of output has risen strongly during the present upswing. From the beginning of 1998 up to the third quarter of 1999, 1 030 000 jobs were created according to the Labour Force Survey. Several factors explain booming employment. First, the demand for labour has been supported by moderate wage claims, by cuts in non-wage labour costs for targeted workers under new permanent contracts (with reduced severance payments and lower social security contributions) and by several features of the 1997 labour market reform.[2] Specifically, almost two million permanent contracts were signed between January 1998 and October 1999, two thirds of which benefited from reduced non-wage costs (one third were conversions from temporary to the new permanent, and subsidised, contracts). Even though permanent contracts rose strongly, the share of workers under fixed-term contracts has remained broadly stable since 1997, at around 33 per cent of total employment. In part, this reflects a rapid increase in fixed-term contracts in the public sector, in particular at the territorial level where the 1 to 4 replacement rule was particularly difficult to respect (Figure 4, panel A).[3] Furthermore, the share of temporary contracts tends to rise during upswings, as the restrictive employment legislation does not apply to them. Second, labour-intensive sectors have been the main driving forces of economic growth. Specifically, 92 per cent of net jobs created from the beginning of 1998 up to the third quarter of 1999 were in the service (in particular tourism-related activities) and construction sectors. Third, part-time employment has risen steeply after the introduction of a new, subsidised, part-time contract in January 1999, though from a low level by international standards (around 8 per cent compared with 16 per cent on average in the European Union). Overall, these trends in employment have been reflected in a poor evolution of apparent productivity. Fourth, the personal income tax reform has raised small entrepreneurs' incentives to hire.

Despite important progress in reforming product and labour markets in the past decade and a sharp rise in investment in physical and human capital, aggregate measured labour productivity growth has slowed down since 1995 (Figure 5). In other OECD countries, the current expansion has also been labour intensive, and been accompanied by a slow down in productivity (France, Italy and the Netherlands). However, rapid job creation is not necessarily incompatible with high productivity growth, as the Irish and Finnish cases demonstrate. To some extent, low productivity growth in Spain may reflect measurement problems of employment and/or output (Box 1). However, it could also reflect slow growth in underlying productivity. Higher labour productivity growth is important in the long term since it determines per capita income, although Spain could grow quickly for several years by raising its employment ratio to the OECD average. Furthermore, significant wage moderation should be maintained to prevent the

Figure 4. **Employment and unemployment: some key features**

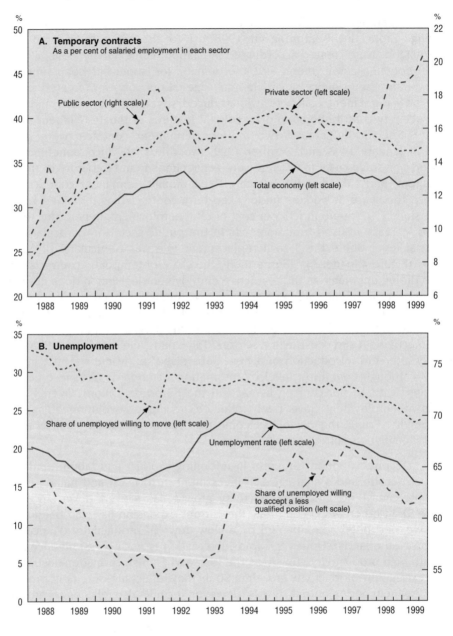

Source: National Institute of Statistics (INE).

Figure 5.   **Productivity growth by sector**

With employment measured by the Labour Force Survey (EPA) and by National Accounts

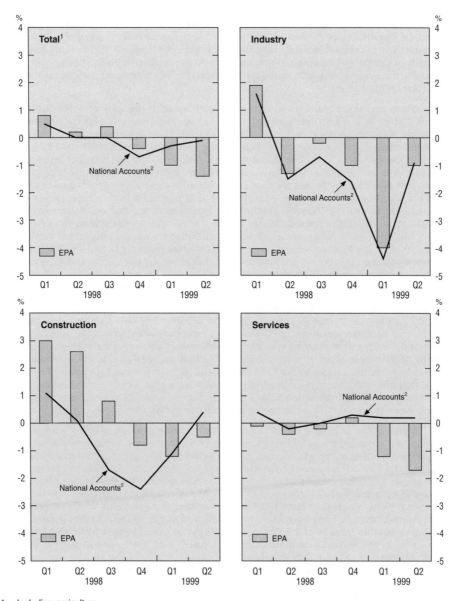

1. Including agriculture.
2. National accounts employment is corrected for the share of part-time work.
Source: National Institute of Statistics (INE).

Box 1. The productivity puzzle: measurement issues

Apparent labour productivity growth has slowed down since 1995, and has even become negative since the last quarter of 1998. At the same time, the *level* of apparent productivity in Spain is considerably above the United Kingdom's and broadly equal to that of Germany. This result, which would seem inconsistent with most indicators of relative development, is most probably accounted for by a significant underestimation of total employment.*

There are three main data sources for employment: the Labour Force Survey (EPA), which is used for international comparisons; social security registrations; and the new National Accounts series (which is calculated using information from EPA and other statistics). Total employment ranged in the second quarter of 1999 from 13.7 million in the EPA, to 15.3 million in the National Accounts. The high level of apparent productivity and the large gap between existing measures of employment may indicate that EPA underestimates the true level of employment. Employment growth also differs significantly across data sources, and this produces large discrepancies in measured productivity changes. Employment growth since the implementation of the 1997 Labour Act to the second quarter of 1999 varies from 7.9 per cent in the EPA to 13.6 per cent when using social security registrations. Overall, output per worker measured by the National Accounts employment series presents both a low level and a more positive evolution of productivity than that shown by the Labour Force Survey, though productivity deteriorates in both cases.

Three factors could explain the under-measurement of productivity growth. *First,* there is some evidence that underground employment has shifted into the formal labour market more rapidly than in previous upturns, boosted by the substantial reduction of social security contributions for new permanent contracts, which has lowered the cost of registering employment. All sources show that the highest growth rates of employment were recorded in construction and services, which are usually considered as the sectors where the underground economy is most prevalent. Part of the shift from the underground economy may also have raised employment measured by the EPA (where information comes directly from households), and therefore may have been reflected in lower apparent productivity growth.

Second, at the beginning of 1999 some methodological changes were implemented in the EPA following Eurostat regulations. One of these changes is the increase in the number of census areas, which could have affected the amount of recorded employment if the new areas covered have lower unemployment rates (for instance, recently urbanised areas that include people with the means to pay for a new house, who are likely to be employed). Another is the introduction of telephone interviews instead of personal visits, which may record higher employment in households where all members work. Statistical factors are likely to be reflected in a level shift of employment in the first quarter (growth of 3.9 per cent), while very large changes have also been recorded in the second and third quarters (4.7 per cent). The seasonal pattern and sampling period changes may also have affected the results of the second and third quarters. To assess the impact of these methodological changes, more observations are needed. In any case, these changes can not account for the already poor productivity performance in 1998.

(continued on next page)

(continued)

Finally, output growth could also be underestimated. In particular, several indicators point to an exceptional strength of private consumption growth. Car registrations and consumer credit have grown at two-digit rates since 1997. Furthermore, indirect tax proceeds rose by close to 13 per cent in the first 10 months of 1999, twice much as the reported growth in private consumption. In addition, recorded marginal productivity of capital turns out to be comparatively low in Spain, given the significantly higher investment ratio than in other strongly expanding economies (for instance France, Ireland, USA – Figure 2). This may seem odd in view of the important progress achieved in deregulation and structural reform, reflecting possibly also underestimation of output growth.

---

* Comparisons of productivity levels are based on GDP converted by purchasing power parity exchange rates and on employment data from national Labour Force Surveys.

---

erosion of competitiveness in the context of slow productivity growth. Two main factors could explain the slow down in underlying productivity. *First*, rapid employment growth exhausts equipment capacity, and a decrease in the capital-labour ratio tends to result in lower labour productivity. Capacity utilisation actually peaked in 1998. *Second*, the nature of the employment created since the 1997 labour market reform was implemented could have also played a role. Most of the new employees are likely to have lower work experience than the average or lower skills (young workers are a majority, but also include previously long-term unemployed and unemployed older than 45). The annual entrance into the labour market of 2 to 3 per cent of workers with lower productivity may affect the average level of productivity through a composition effect.[4] These factors should not affect labour productivity growth permanently, insofar as they reflect lack of capital, lack of experience or deterioration of skills as a consequence of long spells of unemployment or inactivity, and may be reversed in the future with productivity growing above trend.

Employment creation has been fully reflected in a sizeable drop in the unemployment rate, from 19.6 per cent in early 1998, to 15.5 in the third quarter of 1999.[5] The participation rate has remained broadly stable at a low level by international standards. This stability, however, masks an increasing recourse to early retirement schemes for males that is offset by a secular rise in the female participation rate. The youth unemployment rate has been particularly sensitive to the improvement in economic conditions. It dropped by almost 10 percentage points since the end of 1997. However, at close to 30 per cent, it remains one of the highest in the OECD area in 1999. On the other hand, the proportion of long-term unemployed has declined slightly, from 55.5 per cent in 1997 to 51.5 per cent

---

Table 3. **Unemployment rate and hourly earnings by region**

	Unemployment rate, per cent		Hourly earnings, change in per cent	
	1997	1999:Q3	1998/97	1999 H1/1998 H1
Andalucía	31.8	26.8	2.7	2.3
Aragón	14.0	7.8	1.9	2.1
Asturias	21.3	17.3	2.8	1.6
Baleares	11.8	6.1	2.0	1.9
Canarias	19.8	15.3	2.7	3.6
Cantabria	20.9	15.4	1.0	1.6
Castilla-La Mancha	18.6	13.9	2.8	2.2
Castilla y Leon	19.4	14.4	3.3	1.7
Cataluña	17.1	9.7	3.1	2.6
Extremadura	29.2	22.9	3.2	2.3
Galicia	18.4	15.4	3.2	3.6
Madrid	18.4	12.5	3.4	2.5
Murcia	19.5	14.0	3.3	3.0
Navarra	10.0	7.5	3.0	2.7
País Vasco	19.1	14.1	2.2	1.7
La Rioja	11.5	8.4	2.6	3.5
Comunidad Valenciana	20.3	15.0	2.5	2.2
Average	**20.8**	**15.4**	**2.8**	**2.6**
Standard deviation	5.58	5.34	0.63	0.68
Coefficient of variation	0.27	0.35	0.22	0.26

Source: National Statistical Institute (INE), Labour Force Survey and Wage Survey.

in the third quarter of 1999. Furthermore, the dispersion of regional unemployment rates has also increased (Table 3), reinforced by a declining trend in the willingness of the unemployed to move (Figure 4, panel B). In the third quarter of 1999, for instance, only 23.8 per cent of the unemployed indicated that they would accept a job if they had to move. This contrasts with the much higher proportion of the unemployed ready to accept lower paid jobs (62.3 per cent). The low regional mobility is reinforced by the fact that 90 per cent of new job contracts are still of a temporary nature.[6] Uncertainty about future incomes combined with persisting rigidities in the housing market (small number of apartments to rent, expensive housing investment, significant variations in prices from one region to another) hamper regional mobility. This in turn contributes to regional shortages of labour. Reflecting the emergence of regional bottlenecks, some regions recently asked for an increase in the number of work permits allocated to foreigners (*e.g.* Galicia and Murcia).

Disinflation has stalled

Despite moderate wage claims and cuts in non-wage costs...

The buoyancy of the labour market in the past three years has not yet put upward pressure on wages at the aggregate level. Expectations of further disinflation and the personal income tax cut in 1999 contributed to the moderation in contractual wage claims and actual settlements have entailed a loss in purchasing power of gross wages from the third quarter of 1999 (Figure 6, panel A). The increase in effective earnings has been even more moderate reflecting the hiring of new workers on lower wages, the removal of seniority bonuses in some sectors, and less recourse to overtime. The increasing number of workers under new permanent contracts, with reduced social security contributions, has further contributed to restrain labour costs. However, with the available slack in the labour market rapidly taken up, wage pressures started to emerge in some activities. Specifically, the wage drift in the construction sector has risen (Figure 6, panel B). Overall, despite low wage growth, even lower aggregate productivity gains have implied an edging up in unit labour costs and, in the manufacturing sector, these have been rising significantly faster than the euro area average.

... the process of disinflation has stalled in 1999

Price inflation – as measured by the headline CPI – edged up in 1999. The hike in oil and food prices, after a severe drought, pushed up the 12-month headline rate from an historically low 1.4 per cent in December 1998 to 2.7 per cent in November 1999. The effective depreciation of the euro in 1999 has put further pressure on import prices which have recovered following their drop in 1998. The underlying rate of inflation has been less volatile. After a rapid fall from 1995 to 1997, it has hovered around 2¼ per cent since 1998 (Figure 7, panel A). This broad stability masks persisting inflation differentials between goods and services, mostly resulting from low competitive pressures in many service sectors (Figure 7, panel B). Specifically, rent and health care price increases have largely outpaced overall inflation, and in the retail trade sector profit margins have edged up. Buoyant demand has also exerted strong inflation pressures in other services, especially in the tourism industry. On the other hand, enhanced competition in the electricity and telecommunication sectors has pushed prices down, though ensuing price cuts may not be fully reflected in the CPI.[7] At the same time, prices of non-energy industrial goods, which are largely exposed to foreign competition, have remained subdued. Overall, however, the inflation differential with the euro area average has widened to 1 percentage point since Spring 1999 (Figure 7, panel C).

Figure 6.   **Wage settlements, total wages and the consumer price index**

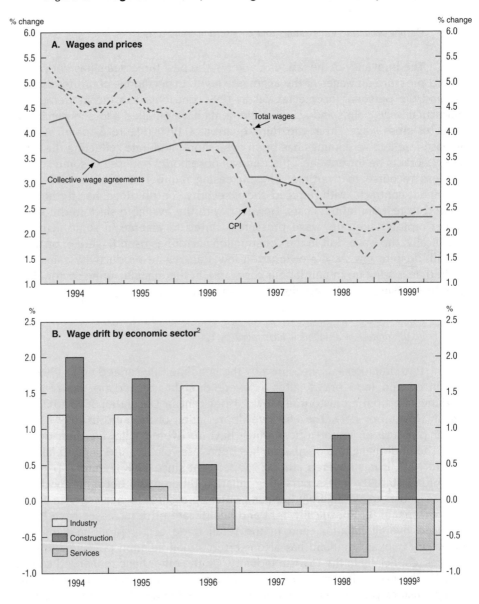

1.   The fourth quarter of 1999 corresponds to October 1999 for the collective wage agreements and the CPI.
2.   Wage drift is calculated as the average increase in earnings less collective agreements.
3.   Second quarter of 1999.
Source: Ministry of Economy and Finance, *Síntesis de Indicatores Económicos* and OECD, *Main Economic Indicators.*

Figure 7. **Consumer prices**
Growth rates

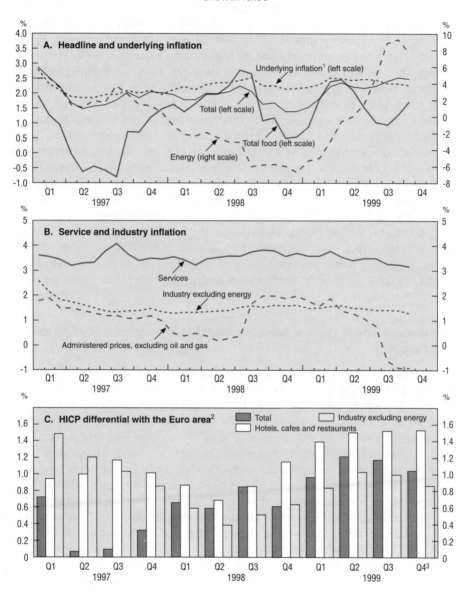

1. Excluding non-processed food and energy.
2. HICP: Harmonised Index of Consumer Prices.
3. October 1999.
Source: Ministry of Economy and Finance.

Spain has maintained a favourable competitive position

The effective depreciation of the euro in 1999 and the continuing decline in corporate financial costs have thus far mitigated the impact on competitiveness stemming from relatively unfavourable unit labour cost developments. Further-more, the high level of corporate profits has allowed exporters to price to market and keep their export prices at a competitive level. Thus, while price inflation of non-energy industrial goods has hovered at around 1.5 per cent on the domestic market since 1998, manufacturing export prices have dropped. Overall, the real effective exchange rate – measured by relative export prices in the manufacturing sector – has depreciated in 1999 (Figure 8, panel A). Further attesting to Spain's high *level* of competitiveness is the strength of FDI inflows, in particular in the highly competitive automotive sector. This reflects not only the still lower level of labour costs but also the sharp rise in human and physical investment over the past decade, and the improvement in infrastructure more recently. As a result, Spain is gradually diversifying its production and export base towards higher quality products. Similar trends characterise the tourism industry where, despite higher inflation, Spain has succeeded in gaining market shares over the past decade. This also partly results from past promotional efforts to diversify the demand towards alternative destinations and to spread visitor stays out of the peak summer season.

... but divergences in cyclical positions have led to a deterioration in the current account

The combination of booming domestic demand and sluggish export mar-kets since the second half of 1998 have led to a significant deterioration in the trade deficit. Though this was partly offset by another record tourist season, the current account moved into slight deficit in 1998, after rising surpluses from 1995, and further widened to 0.8 per cent of GDP in the first eight months of 1999 (Table 4). Import growth mirrored developments in private consumption and equipment investment. In addition, relatively high capacity utilisation and a shift in demand towards goods for which Spain has no supply, *e.g.* sport utility vehicles, magnified the import response to growing demand. As a matter of fact, imports of equipment and non-food consumer goods both rose by around 20 per cent in the first 9 months of 1999. Concerning exports, the marked slowdown in industrial production, coupled with destocking, in most EU countries severely affected Spanish exports of goods, 45 per cent of which are intermediate goods (Figure 8, panel B). Furthermore, exports to Latin America, which account for around 7 per cent of total exports of goods, plunged in the aftermath of the emerging market crisis after being one of the most dynamic export components. Overall, the growth of Spain's export markets more than halved between the first half of 1998 and the first half of 1999. Adding to the demand shock, a severe drought in Spain hit food

Figure 8. **External competitiveness, EU industrial production
and Spanish exports**

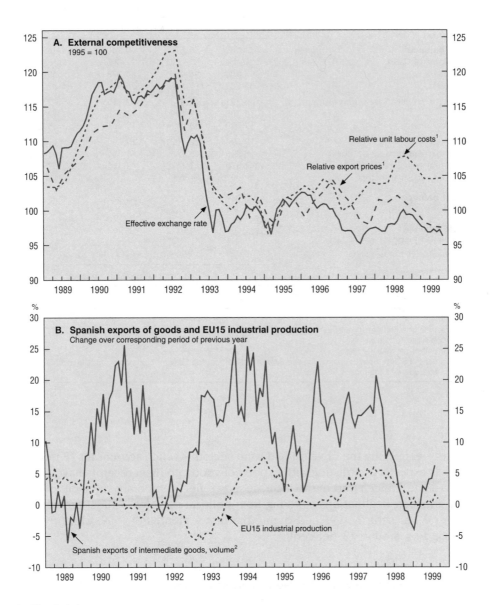

1. Manufacturing.
2. Three-month moving average.
Source: OECD Secretariat and OECD, *Main Economic Indicators.*

Table 4. **The current and capital accounts of the balance of payments**

	1997	1998	Jan.-Aug. 1998	Jan.-Aug. 1999
	Million euros			
Trade balance[1]	−11 587	−16 676	−9 140	−16 027
(per cent of GDP)	−2.4	−3.2	−2.6	−4.3
Exports	93 700	98 485	65 378	65 973
Imports	105 287	115 160	74 518	82 000
Non-factor services (excluding tourism)	−2 721	−3 312	−2 115	−2 391
Credits	15 208	17 179	11 336	12 844
Debits	17 929	20 491	13 451	15 234
Tourism	19 694	22 302	15 094	17 096
Net investment income outflows[2]	−5 910	−6 746	−4 565	−4 833
Net current transfers	2 570	3 163	3 345	2 910
of which: Net EU transfers	997	1 260	..	..
Current balance	2 047	−1 269	2 620	−3 245
(per cent of GDP)	0.4	−0.2	0.8	−0.9
Capital balance	5 606	5 624	3 962	3 663
(per cent of GDP)	1.1	1.1	1.1	1.0
of which: Net EU transfers	3 929	4 963	..	..
	Per cent change, annual rate			
Terms of trade, goods and services[3]	−0.4	1.1	−1.0[4]	1.5[4]

1. F.o.b.
2. Investment and labour income.
3. National accounts basis.
4. First half of the year.
Source: Bank of Spain, *Boletín Económico and Boletín Estadístico*, and Ministry of Economy and Finance, *Síntesis de Indicadores Económicos*.

exports – especially the olive oil and wine sectors – which account for 12 per cent of goods exports. Contrasting with exports of goods, tourism receipts have continued to surge, though part of the increase may reflect temporary shifts out of other Mediterranean destinations suffering from political troubles. Tourist arrivals rose by over 9 per cent in 1998 and during the first 9 months of 1999, while receipts increased by around 13 per cent.

Macroeconomic policy: supportive of output growth

Until 1998, macroeconomic policy was geared towards meeting the Maastricht criteria, to secure Spain's membership in monetary union. The fiscal consolidation efforts were particularly strong in 1996 and 1997. The budget deficit

Table 5. **The process of fiscal consolidation: Spain and the euro area**

As a per cent of GDP

	1995	1996	1997	1998	1999[1]	2000[2]	1996-97	1998-2000
							Compounded change[3]	
Spain								
Net lending	−6.9	−5.0	−3.1	−2.3	−1.4	−1.1	..	..
Changes in net lending	**−0.9**	**1.9**	**1.9**	**0.8**	**0.9**	**0.3**	**3.8**	**2.0**
due to:								
Changes in structural primary balance	−0.1	2.3	1.1	−0.1	0.5	−0.3	3.4	0.1
Cyclical conditions	−0.2	−0.3	0.2	0.5	−0.1	0.1	−0.1	0.5
Changes in interest payments[4]	−0.6	−0.1	0.6	0.4	0.5	0.5	0.5	1.4
Euro area								
Net lending	−4.9	−4.1	−2.6	−2.0	−1.6	−1.2	..	..
Changes in net lending	**0.0**	**0.8**	**1.5**	**0.6**	**0.4**	**0.4**	**2.3**	**1.4**
due to:								
Changes in structural primary balance	0.0	1.2	1.2	−0.1	0.3	0.0	2.4	0.2
Cyclical conditions	0.1	−0.4	0.0	0.3	−0.2	0.2	−0.4	0.3
Changes in interest payments[4]	−0.1	0.0	0.3	0.4	0.3	0.2	0.3	0.9
Memorandum items:								
Real short-term interest rate differential of Spain to the euro area[5]	1.0	1.8	0.6	−0.3	−1.0	−0.7	1.2	−0.7
Output gap, Spain	−1.5	−2.0	−1.0	0.3	0.2	0.7	−1.5	0.4
Output gap, euro area	−1.0	−1.6	−1.4	−0.8	−1.1	−0.6	−1.5	−0.8

1. OECD Secretariat estimates.
2. OECD Secretariat projections.
3. Average for memorandum items.
4. Positive numbers indicate a decrease in interest payments as a share of GDP.
5. In per cent. Computed from 3-month interest rates and actual changes in private consumption deflators.
Source: OECD Secretariat.

was reduced to 3.1 per cent of GDP in 1997 from 6.9 per cent in 1995, while the primary budget surplus increased by 3.4 per cent of GDP (Table 5). Fiscal consolidation was further pursued in the 1998-2000 budgets, though at a slower pace, with the 2000 budget targeting a deficit-to-GDP ratio of 0.8 per cent. The adjustment effort over 1996-97 relied largely on cuts in primary expenditure, hence making a long lasting budget consolidation more likely and laying the ground for the 1999 personal income tax reform. Successful fiscal adjustment enhanced the credibility of the commitment to participate in the euro area from the outset and prompted a sharp decline in interest rates by reducing interest-rate spreads with core euro area economies. This boosted investment expenditures. Moreover, due to the shrinking public sector borrowing requirement, a larger part of financial resources were funnelled to firms and households, further facilitating the boom in private investment and consumption.[8] The expectation of reduced future tax liabilities, due to fiscal consolidation, may have also induced positive wealth effects. Monetary conditions have become exceptionally easy, especially after the European Central Bank reduced interest rates in April 1999, coming on top of the depreciation of the euro. With inflation above the euro-area average, monetary conditions are even easier in Spain. The real short-term interest rate, for instance, is lower than in the euro area (Table 5). With the inflation differential *vis-à-vis* the euro area rising since 1998, this discrepancy in real interest rates has been increasing further. Hence, with the economy's cyclical position already well ahead of the euro area average – as evidenced by the positive output gap which has appeared since 1998 – monetary conditions seem to have turned overly expansionary.

Fiscal policy: a slowing pace of fiscal consolidation

Since 1998 the pace of fiscal consolidation has slowed, with the primary budget surplus projected to increase by only 0.6 percentage points of GDP over the three fiscal exercises from 1998 to 2000. The improvement is almost entirely due to the cycle, with only a 0.1 per cent of GDP increase in the structural primary budget surplus (Table 5). Nevertheless, owing to lower debt service payments amounting to 1.4 per cent of GDP – as a result of lower interest rates, improved debt management and a declining debt-to-GDP ratio – the actual budget deficit is projected to decline by 2 percentage points from 1998 to 2000. This pattern of fiscal consolidation parallels that in the euro area, where discretionary adjustment has come to a halt over 1998-2000 as well (Table 5). From 1996 to 1997, Spain needed to carry out bolder fiscal adjustment than in the euro area, as it started from a less favourable situation with a sizeable fiscal deficit. From 1998 to 2000 Spain is ahead of the euro area in terms of its cyclical position, as evidenced by the positive output gap which is projected to increase to nearly 0.7 per cent of GDP in 2000. The opportunity provided by this favourable position should be seized, to achieve a more ambitious fiscal consolidation than in the rest of the euro area. In fact, this will be examined in the context of Spain's revised Stability Programme.

The fiscal dividend from stronger growth has been largely dedicated to finance the introduction of a major personal income tax reform, included in the 1999 budget. The tax reform (reviewed in the special chapter) aimed to stream-line the tax system, alleviate the rising tax burden on labour income, and reduce tax rates. The 1999 income tax cuts were also funded by various discretionary measures, such as the restraint on the civil servants' wage bill – reflecting the rule of replacing only one in four retiring civil servants – and by better tax collection, especially of VAT, owing to improved tax compliance.[9] On the expenditure side, from 1998 on, fiscal policy shifted primary spending towards public investment. Net capital outlays, which had been compressed substantially in recent years, dropping by 1.2 per cent as a share of GDP from 1995 to 1997, will recover by 0.4 per cent in the three fiscal exercises from 1998 to 2000. The budget outcomes have been better than targeted, partly due to healthy growth but also thanks to rigorous management of the budget.

The 1999 and 2000 budgets

The implementation of the 1999 budget has been on track and the deficit is projected by the OECD to drop below the 1.6 per cent initial target. The deficit of the central government is projected at around 1 per cent of GDP, while the accounts of social security should be broadly balanced and the deficit of other public entities and territorial administrations should reach 0.3 per cent of GDP. As a result of the tax reform, personal income tax revenues are projected to decline in 1999, reducing direct tax pressure on households by around ³/₄ percentage points of GDP (Table 6).[10] The shortfall in personal income tax revenues has been more than offset by the buoyancy of other taxes, especially consumption-based taxes, due to strong growth in domestic demand and healthy corporate profits.[11] Moreover, revenue from social security contributions has outperformed the targets due to strong employment growth and the favourable trend in social security registrations. On the expenditure side, the execution of the budget has been broadly on track, with overruns at the state level occurring only in consumption of goods and services and in public investment. An overrun in interest payments during the first half of 1999 resulted mainly from the concentration of public debt maturing in the early months of the year and should be reversed in the second half.

The 2000 budget aims at a further decline in the general government's deficit to 0.8 per cent of GDP, which is below the 1 per cent deficit target in Spain's first Stability Programme for 1998-2002. The central government's deficit is also projected at 0.8 per cent of GDP, while a slight social security budget surplus of 0.1 per cent of GDP would be offset by a projected deficit of other public entities and territorial administrations. The projected decline in the deficit-to-GDP ratio should stem mostly from reduced payments on debt service (up to 0.5 per cent of GDP), while the cycle also leads to some improvement (Table 5). According to the OECD Secretariat's projections, the structural primary surplus is estimated to fall by 0.3 percentage points of GDP, leading to weaker fiscal consolidation than foreseen in the budget, and signalling a broadly supportive fiscal stance. The projected decline in the structural surplus reflects programmed maintenance of social spending, increases in infrastructure investment, the effects

Table 6. **General government accounts**

National accounts definition, per cent of GDP

	1995	1996	1997	1998	1999[1]	2000[2]
Current receipts, total	**35.5**	**36.3**	**36.8**	**37.1**	**37.2**	**36.9**
Direct taxes	10.1	10.3	10.5	10.3	9.7	9.5
Household direct taxes	8.1	8.2	7.7	7.6	6.9	6.6
Corporate direct taxes	2.0	2.1	2.8	2.7	2.8	2.8
Indirect taxes	10.2	10.2	10.5	11.1	11.7	11.7
Social security contributions	13.0	13.2	13.2	13.2	13.3	13.4
Other	2.2	2.6	2.5	2.6	2.4	2.3
Current disbursements, total	**39.2**	**39.1**	**37.8**	**37.1**	**36.2**	**35.5**
Government consumption	18.1	18.0	17.6	17.4	17.1	16.9
of which: Wages and salaries	11.3	11.3	10.9	10.7	10.5	10.3
Subsidies	1.1	1.0	0.9	1.2	1.2	1.2
Social security outlays	13.9	13.8	13.4	13.0	12.8	12.7
Property income paid	5.2	5.4	4.8	4.4	3.9	3.4
Other	0.9	1.0	1.1	1.2	1.2	1.2
Saving	−3.6	−2.8	−1.0	0.0	1.0	1.4
Net capital outlays	3.3	2.2	2.1	2.3	2.4	2.5
Net lending	−6.9	−5.0	−3.1	−2.3	−1.4	−1.1
Memorandum items:						
Net primary balance	−2.4	−0.2	1.3	1.7	2.1	2.0

1.   OECD estimates.
2.   OECD projections.
Source: Data submitted by national authorities and OECD Secretariat.

from the 1999 personal income tax cuts spreading into 2000, and revenue shortfalls from tax freezes and rebates included in the budget. The impact of these measures would be only partly offset by the maintenance of the hiring restrictions for civil servants and by assuming a further improvement in VAT tax compliance.

On the revenue side, the excise taxes on fuels, tobacco and alcohol will be frozen at their 1999 rates, rather than being raised by projected inflation, as in the past, to reduce cost pressures. Moreover, butane gas cylinders, which account for a significant share of household energy consumption, will be taxed at a lower 7 per cent VAT rate – rather than at 16 per cent. The VAT on some minor household items and labour-intensive services will also be reduced from 16 to 7 per cent. The unemployment insurance contribution rates for both employers and employees will be reduced by 0.25 percentage points. The cost of this measure should be largely covered by buoyant employment growth. Finally corporate income tax breaks for investment in R&D will be further enhanced, with the aim of bringing Spain's comparatively low share of R&D investment closer to the EU average.[12]

On the expenditure side, the budget targets three priority areas: *i*) Stepping up investment in core infrastructure, which is set to increase by 7.7 per cent, against a budgeted increase of 6.0 per cent in total primary outlays of the general government; *ii*) Enhancing public investment spending in R&D, which should increase by 10.5 per cent; *iii*) Strengthening active labour market policies, with expenditures in this area granted a 9 per cent increase. Total spending in these three areas is projected to rise to 7.6 per cent of central government expenditures, up from 7.3 per cent in 1999. Concerning outlays for social purposes, the budget aims to distribute the benefits from improved economic performance widely. It thus raises spending on entitlement programmes for targeted groups of the population – specifically the minimum pensions (which will cost an estimated ESP 61 billion) and the benefits for long-term unemployed older than 45 years (ESP 50 billion). Reflecting the commitments of the *Toledo Pact*, the 2000 budget completes the separation of financing for non-contributive and contributive benefits, to be covered respectively by the state and the social security. As a consequence, the share of social security spending covered by the state is set to rise to 34.7 per cent – and this also explains the slight social security surplus projected for 2000. Finally, the budget created a reserve fund, with an initial endowment of ESP 60 billions (0.07 per cent of GDP), that is set to partly cover the unfunded liabilities of the pay-as-you-go pension system.[13]

A tighter fiscal policy stance would reduce overheating risks

Aiming at a faster pace of fiscal consolidation would help secure the favourable growth prospects of the economy. Underlying demand pressures may induce costs rising faster than in the euro area, while past favourable cost developments, which in recent years have mitigated the effect on prices of fairly high growth in unit labour costs, are likely to be reversed. In the current context, the scope for a further decline in firms' financial and non-wage labour costs is low, while the higher headline inflation rate in recent months could raise wage costs, as a large share of wage settlements contains an indexation clause. Moreover, the tightening labour market might heighten wage claims. Adverse domestic cost developments may weaken competitiveness and be reflected in an even sharper widening of the current account deficit. This would eventually put the sustainability of recent strong employment and output growth at risk. Tightening fiscal policy would help rebalance the policy mix and forestall demand pressures, as the stance of the single monetary policy in the euro area – despite the projected tightening in the two years ahead – is unlikely to fit well the more advanced cyclical position of the Spanish economy. This would thus hold back the risks of overheating. In addition, moderate wage agreements should ensure that labour cost developments are kept in line with the euro area, thus safeguarding competitiveness.

The case for further tightening the fiscal stance would become even stronger if the 1 percentage point increase in the inflation differential with the euro area since early 1998 turned out to reflect pressures from excess demand rather than structural inflation.[14] A structural inflation differential does not necessarily lead to a loss of competitiveness, if higher wage costs are offset by strong productivity growth in the traded goods sector, thus holding back increases in unit labour costs. It would not, thus, necessarily call for macroeconomic policy tightening. Nevertheless, recent productivity trends in Spain (Box 1), especially starting from the fourth quarter of 1998, point to an even slower productivity growth in industry than in services and construction. This development should be closely monitored before drawing firm conclusions – as it may have been influenced by rapidly receding labour market slack and as it has been plagued by measurement problems.

Medium-term challenges for fiscal consolidation

Looking forward, beyond the 2000 budget, Spain's Stability Programme – approved by the European Commission in early 1999 – indicates further consolidation and a slight surplus of 0.1 per cent of GDP by 2002. The major part of the adjustment effort is to come from the central government budget, whose projected deficit of 1.3 per cent of GDP in 1999 is to be turned into a 0.1 per cent surplus in 2002. The social security budget is projected to remain in balance, while the territorial administrations should also share part of the effort, with their 0.2 per cent estimated deficit in 1999 being removed as from 2001. Fiscal consolidation would be achieved by further reining in primary government expenditure, so as to hold back the tax burden. The debt-to-GDP ratio is seen as falling below 60 per cent by 2002. Spain's fiscal consolidation target is among the more ambitious in the European Union (Table 7). Moreover, reflecting better-than-projected results for 1999, the projected deficit path could be revised downwards in the updated Stability Programme, leading to a further slight increase in the budget surplus target in 2002.

Meeting the balanced budget target by 2002, as stated in Spain's Stability Programme, while keeping the tax burden from rising, involves an additional effort in cutting primary expenditure, – around ¾ percentage points of GDP over the next three years on Secretariat estimates. Savings in public outlays could mainly be expected from four sources: i) further cuts in the wage bill, resulting from the maintenance of the hiring restrictions of civil servants – though the rule has been softened for the hiring of local authorities' employees; ii) further downsizing of transfers to public utilities (railways, urban transport, postal service, broadcasting); iii) lower outlays for unemployment benefits as the slack in the labour market recedes further; iv) better management of health services that

Table 7. **Budget deficit projections in the Stability and Convergence Programmes**

General government surplus (+)/deficit (−) (per cent of GDP)

	1997	1998	1999	2000	2001	2002
Spain	**−2.6**	**−1.9**	**−1.6**	**−1.0**	**−0.4**	**0.1**
Austria	−1.9	−2.2	−2.0	−1.7	−1.5	−1.4
Belgium	−1.9	−1.6	−1.3	−1.0	−0.7	−0.3
Denmark	0.5	1.1	2.5	2.8	2.6	(¹)
Finland	−1.1	1.1	2.4	2.2	2.1	2.3
France²	−3.0	−2.9	−2.2	−1.8	−1.6	−1.2
Germany	−2.7	−2½	−2	−2	−1½	−1
Greece	−4.0	−2.4	−2.1	−1.7	−0.8	. .
Ireland	0.9	2.0/1.7³	1.7	1.4	1.6	. .
Italy	−2.7	−2.6	−2.4	−1.5	−1.0	−0.6
Luxembourg	2.9	2.1	1.1	1.2	1.3	1.7
Netherlands	−0.9	−1.3	−1.3	. .	. .	−1.1⁴
Portugal	. .	. .	−2.0	−1.5	−1.2	−0.8
Sweden	−0.8	1.5	0.3	1.6	2.5	. .
United Kingdom⁵	−0.6	0.8	−0.3	−0.3	−0.1	0.2⁶
Euro area	**−2.5**	**−2.3**	**−1.8**	**−1.6**	**−1.1**	**−0.8**
EU-15	**−2.4**	**−1.7**	**−1.4**	**−1.2**	**−0.8**	**−0.5**

1.   Surplus of 3.5 per cent of GDP projected for 2005.
2.   Prudent scenario. Deficits of 1.7 per cent, 1.2 per cent and 0.8 per cent of GDP over the period 2000-2002 in the favourable scenario.
3.   ESA-1979 basis for 1997 and 1998. ESA-1995 basis for 1998 (second figure) and subsequent years.
4.   Cautious scenario. Deficit of ¼ per cent of GDP and surplus of ¼ per cent in 2002 under middle and favourable scenario respectively.
5.   The figures provided in the United Kingdom's convergence programme are on a financial year basis.
6.   Surplus of 0.1 per cent of GDP projected for the financial year 2003-2004.
Source: National Stability and Convergence Programmes and European Commission services.

could result from recent reforms – though stronger health care demand, due to population ageing, could in the long run offset these savings.

On the other hand, medium-term pressures on the budget that may more than offset the projected savings could result from at least three sources: *i*) increased public investment outlays to upgrade core infrastructure. This is needed to enhance productivity and further promote regional development;[15] *ii*) the needed reduction in the tax wedge on labour income, via reduced social security contributions on the low-paid (see Chapter III); *iii*) higher pension liabilities, due to population ageing (see Chapter II). Though there is some scope to reduce labour taxes by shifting the tax mix to indirect taxes (which are low by international comparison), an increase in indirect taxes might not be easy to implement if wage settlements were to be indexed to higher consumer prices, thus burdening labour costs.[16] On the other hand, if the rates of social security contributions were to be reduced, this would add to the need of reform of the pension system to address the resulting financing needs. On balance, though the additional effort needed to hit the target of a balanced budget by 2002 might seem relatively small, the underlying structural pressures on the budget will be long-lasting and are set to become progressively more acute in the medium term. To accommodate these pressures, at least partly, while further reducing the tax wedge on labour, more ambitious savings in public outlays will be needed, especially in pension and health care entitlement programmes, as well as in support provided to public utilities.

Seizing the opportunity of strong growth prospects to further step up the pace of fiscal consolidation would also provide more room for fiscal manoeuvre under the EU's Stability and Growth Pact (SGP). According to OECD Secretariat calculations, the budget deficit in Spain is estimated to widen by nearly 0.5 per cent of GDP when output deviates from potential by 1 percentage point.[17] This is close to the average cyclical sensitivity of budget deficits in the OECD zone. The projected medium-term path of budget deficits should provide a wide enough margin to allow fiscal stabilisers to operate while complying with the Stability and Growth Pact in case of moderate slowdowns. Given the historical pattern of cyclical disturbances, a cyclically-adjusted budget deficit somewhat below 1 per cent would provide Spain with a 90 per cent confidence margin of complying with the 3 per cent deficit limit over a three to five year horizon, without resorting to pro-cyclical fiscal tightening (Dalsgaard and De Serres, 1999). While the cyclically-adjusted budget deficits projected by the Secretariat in 2000 and 2001 are close to this "safety margin", a further effort is called for to comply effectively with the SGP. Moreover, a recession as severe as that experienced in the early 1990s could lead to "excessive deficits", breaching the 3 per cent limit of the SGP. Aiming at more ambitious consolidation targets would be needed not only to allow fiscal stabilisers to operate while securing compliance with the SGP, but also to allow more scope for discretionary fiscal policy to counter adverse shocks. With the loss of monetary policy to smooth cyclical developments, this has increased in importance in the new EMU policy setting.

Securing fiscal discipline at the sub-national levels of government

Territorial governments have shared a significant part of the fiscal adjustment effort.[18] While in 1994 their consolidated budget deficit amounted to 1.1 per cent of GDP, in 1998 it had come down to 0.2 per cent of GDP. This is also reflected in the regional governments' debt-to-GDP ratio, which after rising steeply from 2.7 per cent in 1991 to 5.8 per cent in 1995, progressively stabilised. It reached 6.3 per cent in 1998 (i.e. nearly 10 per cent of total public debt), down from 6.5 per cent in 1997. However, progress in keeping debt dynamics in check has been uneven across regions (Figure 9). The new financing system for the regions, that is due to be discussed in 2001 and become effective over 2002-06, would need to further enhance the incentives for expenditure restraint by

Figure 9. **Debt of regional administrations**
As a per cent of regional GDP

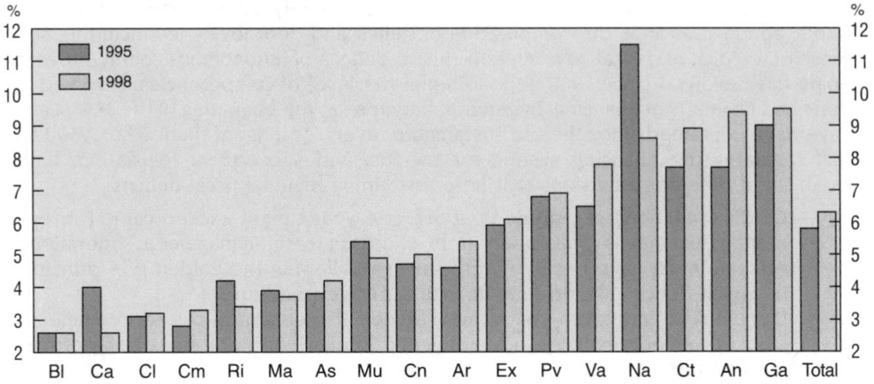

Note: An: Andalucía, Ar: Aragón, As: Asturias, Bl: Baleares, Cn: Canarias, Ca: Cantabria, Cm: Castilla-La Mancha, Cl: Castilla y León, Ct: Cataluña, Ex: Extremadura, Ga: Galicia, Ri: Rioja, Ma: Madrid, Mu: Murcia, Na: Navarra, Pv: País Vasco, Va: Comunidad Valenciana.
Source: Bank of Spain, Statistical Bulletin.

regional governments and their commitment to fiscal discipline. This will ensure that increasing fiscal decentralisation does not put the national fiscal consolidation targets at risk and, thereby, Spain's compliance with the EU's Stability and Growth Pact.

As explained in greater detail in Chapter III, enhancing incentives for expenditure restraint by regional authorities involves matching their rising spending competencies by more extended responsibilities for raising taxes, so as to reduce reliance on transfers from central government that soften their budget constraint. Moreover, assigning broader tax bases to regional governments would reduce the volatility of their tax revenues and allow an easier transition to a lower level of resource guarantees. Currently, to enhance fiscal discipline, the regional governments' borrowing policies are subject to legal constraints and, in addition, have to be consistent with the overall policy objectives on fiscal deficits at the national level. Co-ordination of fiscal policies is implemented within the CPFF ("*Consejo de Política Fiscal y Financiera*"), which sets four-year targets for regional governments' deficits and debt, and is monitored on a bilateral basis by the government and each region (Box 2).

Improving transparency, to allow an effective monitoring of borrowing policies of regional governments, could enhance the current system. In the *first* place, timely public information on the financial positions of sub-national authorities is needed. The Bank of Spain publishes the consolidated financial position of

---

Box 2. Borrowing constraints for regional and local administrations

The Maastricht criteria for nominal convergence rely on a broad definition of public administration in the computation of deficit and debt levels, by including also those of regional and local governments. Fiscal deficits of autonomous communities in Spain have evolved since 1980 depending on the level of competencies devolved to them and channels of financing. In general, they rose at the beginning of the 1990s, and have been contained since then to sustainable levels for most of them. The 1980 Law that regulates the financing system for regions, and subsequent legislation, have established different provisions that help restraining regional fiscal deficits:

- Credit operations of maturities above one year cannot exceed capital investment. This means that, apart from short-run cash management operations, budgets must have positive gross savings, following the golden rule principle by which deficits should only finance capital expenditure.
- Debt service in a given year cannot exceed 25 per cent of current revenues.
- Debt issues of regional governments and foreign borrowing must be approved by the State.

Local governments face similar restrictions on their budget balances and debt levels. In particular:

- Short term credit operations can only finance transitory cash management shortfalls, and should not exceed 30 per cent of current revenues of the previous year.
- New credit operations need the approval of the State when there has been negative net saving in the final budget of the previous year, or when debt levels exceed 110 per cent of current revenues. For large local governments, where debt is concentrated, these approvals may require the presentation of debt consolidation plans, which must be endorsed by the central government.

However, existing rules on deficit and debt restraint are not fully binding for regional governments, since governments that surpass ceilings are difficult to penalise. Non-authorisation of credit by the central government has been the only tool to penalise territorial governments. However, apart from debt issues, finance can be obtained through bank loans, though this source has become more expensive since the level of debt peaked in the early 1990s. Annual programmes of deficit reduction, which are bilaterally negotiated between the State and each region, have been in the end the main factor behind the deficit restraint of regions in recent years.

---

territorial administrations on a timely basis (currently up to 1996), but at present the latest publicly available information on individual regions' budgets on a national account basis dates back to 1994. Nevertheless, some evidence on underlying deficit trends can be obtained from data on debt of regional governments published regularly by the Bank of Spain, though there is no tight matching of deficits and changes in net debt. Second, the fiscal programmes agreed upon in the CPFF by the central government and the regional governments should be made public, to enhance accountability and improve monitoring of fiscal performance. Third, more transparency would seem desirable on the financial relationships between regional governments and local public enterprises. On the one hand, capital transfers to these enterprises that are off budget obscure the net financial position of territorial administrations. On the other hand, local public enterprises are not subject to borrowing restrictions and may borrow from banks under the implicit guarantee that capital transfers from regional governments would be forthcoming to cover their liabilities. Funds raised in this way by local public enterprises may in turn be funnelled to regional governments to finance investment projects, thus making it possible to partly overcome borrowing ceilings and further blurring the transparency of regional budgets.[19]

Further ahead, there is a need to better enforce commitments to fiscal discipline by regional governments since the existing rules for deficit and debt control are not fully enforceable, and there are no penalties in case a region fails to comply with them (Box 2). Better enforcement could be sought by implementing an internal stability pact, imposing deficit limits on regional governments. This would call for a clear definition of fiscal deficit targets or acceptable deficit ceilings, and should ideally include a system of sanctions in case of slippage. Nevertheless, for such a system to work, the level of central government guarantees would need to be lowered, matched by a wider range of tax powers transferred to the regions or a broader sharing of regional tax collections. A shortcoming of systems relying on strict deficit rules, which do not allow an escape in exceptional circumstances, is a lack of flexibility to deal with region-specific shocks, since in that case the application of sanctions may act in a pro-cyclical way. Moreover, they provide unbalanced incentives for fiscal consolidation, since they penalise fiscal slippage without properly rewarding sound fiscal management. Finally, selectivity in the application of penalties may impair the transparency of the system. Alternative market-based mechanisms to enforce fiscal discipline could be considered. Some federal systems function quite well since the markets themselves impose considerable discipline when local government borrowing is not underpinned by guarantees. Another – perhaps radical and difficult to implement – example would be the creation of a market for "tradable budget deficit permits". As in the case of a scheme setting deficit ceilings, such a mechanism recognises that fiscal policy slippage creates negative externalities by putting aggregate financial stability at risk. However, as in the case of market-based schemes of environmental regulation through tradable pollution permits, the rationale is to achieve a global deficit target as efficiently as possible, by minimising total compliance costs (Box 3). Such a mechanism would require an appropriate institutional setting to be in place.

Prospects

The OECD Secretariat's economic projections (Table 8)[20] suggest that domestic demand will remain strong in a context of supportive macroeconomic

---

Box 3. Workings of a system of "tradable deficit permits"

- A tradable deficit permit scheme has been suggested by Casella (1999), drawing on Coase's (1960) principle of voluntary trading of property rights, and parallels institutional arrangements in markets for tradable pollution permits primarily experimented in the United States. Setting up such a system would involve: *i)* making a decision on an overall deficit ceiling; *ii)* making an initial allocation of deficit permits; *iii)* allowing participant entities (territorial administrations) to freely trade deficit permit holdings; *iv)* clearing the accounts of the system at the end of each exercise, ensuring that each participant entity holds enough permits to cover its reported deficits; *v)* enforcing a system of fines in case participant entities fail to meet their deficit permit requirement.
- Under competitive conditions the price quoted in the market should reflect the price of the right to issue a unit of debt. This should vary according to the strains exerted on the financial balance of the system, given the overall deficit ceiling and the cyclical position. In symmetric slowdowns, when the overall balance is under strain, the price of permits should rise, providing incentives to keep the rising deficits at levels that would not breach the overall ceiling. In case a region suffers an asymmetric shock, where more flexibility is needed, the price of the permits should remain low, as the system is not under strain. This would allow an offsetting increase in the deficit to smooth out the shock at relatively low cost. The system provides rewards for sound fiscal management, by allowing profitable selling of unused deficit permits – at a price that in principle should reflect their value at the best alternative use. This would make it more likely to keep budgets in balance in the long run.
- Safeguards and added flexibility:
  - *i)* To counter short-sighted behaviour, participants in the scheme should not be allowed to borrow against future deficit permit allocations.
  - *ii)* To smooth expected deficits and improve planning, deficit permits might be saved within limits: for example, a deficit could be offset by contemporaneous permit allocations or by unused permits of previous years.
  - *iii)* To improve systemic flexibility, the central government might increase the aggregate supply of permits in case of large symmetric shocks (meaning a temporary rise in the deficit ceiling).
  - *iv)* To reflect the differing indebtedness of participants – and hence their differential impact on aggregate financial fragility – the number of deficit permits required to cover a given amount of deficit could grow in step with each participant's debt ratio.
- The implementation of such a mechanism might, however, be difficult, as it may not be easy to reach an agreement on a fair initial allocation of permits. Safeguards may also need to be introduced to prevent collusive behaviour on the part of big players that may distort prices in the market. Moreover, safeguards would be needed to ensure that regions in economic difficulties facing an election do not use the market as a means to issue more debt.

---

policies. Household demand could ease somewhat as household disposable income decelerates, because of waning stimulus from the personal income tax cut and some slowing of employment growth. However, several factors are expected

Table 8. **Short-term prospects**

	1998	1999	2000	2001
	Per cent change, annual rate			
Private consumption	4.1	4.3	3.9	3.5
Government consumption	2.0	1.6	2.4	2.4
Gross fixed investment	9.2	8.8	8.6	8.5
Total domestic demand	5.0	5.0	4.8	4.6
Exports of goods and services	7.1	6.7	8.0	8.1
Imports of goods and services	11.1	11.5	11.4	11.2
Foreign balance[1]	−1.0	−1.3	−1.1	−1.2
GDP at constant prices	4.0	3.7	3.7	3.5
Household saving ratio[2]	11.0	10.9	10.5	10.1
Employment	3.4	4.5	2.8	2.2
Unemployment rate (per cent)	18.8	15.8	14.0	12.7
Private consumption deflator	2.0	2.3	2.4	2.5
Private sector wage rate	2.3	2.6	3.1	3.4
Unit labour costs, manufacturing	1.6	2.0	2.3	2.4
	Per cent of GDP			
Current external balance	−0.2	−1.1	−2.2	−2.9
Government net lending[3]	−2.3	−1.4	−1.1	−0.7
of which: Primary balance	1.7	2.1	2.0	2.1

1.   Contribution to growth of GDP.
2.   Household saving as a percentage of disposable income.
3.   A minus sign indicates a deficit.
Source: INE, Ministry of Finance and OECD Secretariat.

to prompt a decline in the household saving ratio: households' confidence is still very high and the unemployment rate is falling; the cut in personal income tax is progressively built into household's permanent income; and real interest rates are projected to remain at a low level. Forward looking indicators for business investment also remain positive: business sentiment is recovering briskly after the sharp slide in late 1998 and early 1999, corporate profits are solid and order inflows from abroad are improving. The rise in public investment, in accordance with Spain's Stability programme and the implementation of the Infrastructure Plan from 2000 onwards, should provide a further impetus to domestic demand. With economic prospects for Spain's main trading partners set to improve – reflecting a rise in EU area growth as from the second half of 1999 – exports should gain further momentum. The resulting rapid output growth should continue to support job creation, and the unemployment rate could fall to close to 13 per cent.

With demand continuing to expand at a faster rate than the economy's underlying potential, price and wage pressures could intensify and the current account deteriorate further. Adding to demand side stimulus, cost-push factors could reinforce pressures on inflation. The hike in oil prices is already passing through to consumer prices. The high degree of indexation of the Spanish economy (in particular wages, social expenditures, and transfers to the regions) results in a high sensitivity to the supply shock stemming from the reversal in oil prices. This creates additional pressures on both the budget and corporate costs, and could lead to a further widening in the price differential *vis-à-vis* the euro area. If sustained over a prolonged period of time, the competitiveness of the Spanish economy would suffer. Furthermore, the decline in financial costs, which served to mitigate labour cost pressures, has come to an end, and no further cut in non-wage labour costs is planned.[21] On the wage side, a significant share of collective agreements embodies a catch-up clause for inflation, which will be activated in 1999. In 2000, wage claims will likely increase since the labour market is projected to tighten and inflation expectations are reversing. Moreover, the next round of wage negotiations will take place when the first-round effects of the oil price hike will have fully passed through to consumer prices.

The main risk to the favourable growth outlook concerns the response of wage claims to the evolution of labour market tightness and to the recent rise in inflation. If wages rise faster than projected, this would imply a further boost to demand in the short run. However, this would erode competitiveness and threaten the sustainability of employment growth, and could lead to a hard landing scenario. On the other hand, uncertainty surrounds the behaviour of private consumption. The slippage in inflation and the volatility of the Spanish stock market since early 1999 could lower consumer confidence and household spending.

II. Improving performance by stepping up structural reforms

Spain's economic performance has improved rapidly in recent years. Growth considerably above the OECD average has so far not led to strong inflationary pressures and has allowed a rapid reduction in labour market slack. Unemployment has fallen quickly from a peak of 24 per cent in 1994 to close to 15 per cent currently. Yet, the unemployment rate is still the highest in the OECD, and other countries, which also suffered from very high unemployment in the early 1990s, such as Finland and Ireland, reduced unemployment even faster. Hence high unemployment, especially the large share of long-term unemployed and of workers on fixed-term contracts, remains the major policy concern. Several policy initiatives in recent years have spurred structural change in labour, product and financial markets, contributing to strong growth since 1997. Over the medium term, Spanish GDP per capita has come closer to the EU average (Figure 10), though at a much slower pace than that of Ireland or Portugal. In addition, living standards and productivity are still below the EU average and well below that of the best performing OECD countries. This suggests that there remains ample scope for further product and labour market reforms, which can be expected to speed up per capita GDP convergence. Such moves should be accompanied by tax reform initiatives, which are discussed in Chapter III.

The improved macroeconomic policy environment and strong competitiveness may not suffice to achieve a satisfactory labour market performance in the coming years. The government has a good track record in implementing wide-ranging reforms, including the liberalisation of network industries, the "Toledo Pact" on pensions, labour market reform, the devolution of competencies to lower levels of government, and the public enterprise Modernisation Programme, which aimed at the restructuring and sell-off of public enterprises. Arguably, these reforms have already started to provide a sizeable growth dividend. This chapter monitors these reforms and reviews the scope for further structural reform in the labour, product and financial markets. Keeping up the pace of reform would appear to be critical to alleviate obstacles to strong non-inflationary growth and to achieve a further rapid and lasting labour market improvement.

Figure 10. **Convergence in GDP per capita**
As a per cent of OECD average[1]

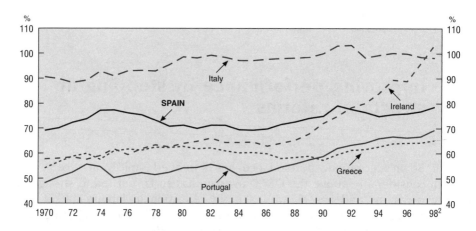

1. Except Czech Republic, Hungary, Poland.
2. Estimates.
Source: OECD, *National Accounts* and OECD Secretariat.

Labour market reform

In assessing Spain's poor labour market performance up to the mid-1990s, it is clear that strict employment protection legislation (EPL) and its interaction with other labour market policies has been a central element. In the mid-1980s, the authorities addressed the rigidities stemming from strict EPL by introducing fixed-term contracts with no firing costs. They have expanded steadily and currently cover one-third of total employment. Because the level of EPL for permanent workers was left unchanged, deregulation of fixed-term contract work has led to a segmented labour market, rather than to a "second best" outcome. Most importantly, expansion of temporary employment – which was largely "involuntary" – has strengthened the bargaining power of those on a permanent contract (insiders), leading to higher wage settlements, and has facilitated forward shifting of taxes into labour costs. This may have increased the cost of disinflation in terms of employment. Moreover, it has weakened job attachment with detrimental effects on training and human capital formation, especially for younger workers. As a result, strict EPL has had little effect on unemployment of core worker groups (prime-age men), but led to a much higher level of unemployment of other groups (youth, women) that are more vulnerable to changes in labour demand.[22]

The impact of employment protection legislation on labour market performance

Stable employment relationships may have a positive effect on productivity, insofar as they may increase training and reinforce the attachment of the worker to the firm, though the international evidence on the relationship between job tenure and training is inconclusive (OECD, 1999f). In Spain, participation in training programmes seems to be weak as compared to other OECD countries,[23] suggesting that the link between EPL and on-the-job training is not strong. In any case, the high recourse to fixed-term employment induced by strict EPL does not provide incentives for workers to embark on firm-specific training programmes by undergoing a period of lower earnings, or for firms to provide general training for their employees. It may even have reduced work effort, since most temporary workers know that they stand a low chance to be kept in the firm.[24]

EPL acts effectively as a tax on labour adjustment, thus reducing labour turnover. In Spain, high levels of EPL have reduced turnover rates for core workers and raised them for "outsiders", since firms have used temporary contracts more as a way of obtaining cheap labour and as a buffer for employment adjustment rather than as a first step towards permanent hiring. Evidence shows that only one quarter of labour turnover in Spain is due to job reallocation (creation and destruction of jobs), while the rest corresponds to the same jobs rotating for different workers (García Serrano and Jimeno, 1998). Legal limitations for chaining temporary contracts have reinforced this tendency, with about a third of workers locked in frequent transitions between temporary jobs or from temporary work to unemployment,[25] experiencing hence difficulties to gain access to more stable careers. Young workers have been especially affected by this phenomenon, with almost 75 per cent of them working under a fixed-term contract (the highest share among a large sample of OECD countries).[26] This sharp segmentation of the labour market not only marginalises part of the labour force, but also affects the performance of the economy. First, low turnover for permanent workers damages the effectiveness of the matching process between workers and occupations and therefore may reduce the level of aggregate productivity. Second, low turnover and high overall unemployment rates increase the incidence of long-term unemployment, which erodes the skills of these workers. In 1998 almost 10 per cent of the Spanish labour force had been unemployed for more than 12 months.

EPL also affects the rate of unemployment through the wage determination process. In flexible labour markets with low firing costs, large imbalances between labour supply and demand are reduced through wage moderation. In Spain, wage pressure started increasing already at the end of the 1980s, when unemployment was still very high – 16 per cent in 1989. The presumed downward pressure on salaries by unemployed workers is not effective, since wage bargaining positions are determined by the majority of insider workers, who are relatively

Table 9. **Empirical evidence on dual labour markets in Spain**

Authors	Data	Equation	Results
Draper (1993)	Period: 1984-89. Disaggregated sectoral data on manufacturing from *Central de Balances* (Bank of Spain).	Wage equation to determine insider power.	Wide range of insider power in different sectors. Metal and chemicals are those with the highest power.
Bentolila and Dolado (1994)	Period: 1983-88. 1 167 manufacturing firms.	Wage equation.	Small but statistically significant effect of insider power. Strong buffer effect of temporary workers.
Jiménez-Martín (1998)	Period: 1984-91. Firm-level manufacturing data.	Wage equation.	Strong evidence of spillover effect from different bargaining levels.
Huguet (1999)	Period: 1991. Survey: *"Encuesta de Estructura, Conciencia y Biografía de Clase"*, 6 632 individuals.	Allocation of workers into segments applying *switching regression model with unknown regimes*.	Clear evidence on the dual labour market hypothesis, with substantial differences in the wage determination process between segments.

Source: OECD Secretariat.

sheltered by EPL from unemployment risks. A large share of fixed-term contracts reinforces this effect, because employment adjustment is likely to affect primarily temporary workers with no firing costs (Bentolila and Dolado, 1994). Although real wage increases have kept pace with aggregate productivity growth since the mid-1980s, there is considerable microeconomic evidence showing that strict EPL together with a wage bargaining structure centred at the sector level has impeded the adjustment of real wages to productivity conditions at the firm level (Table 9). Furthermore, part of the moderation of aggregate average wages comes from a composition effect – *i.e.* lower wages paid to temporary workers compensating high increases for core workers as the temporary share grows, as it has happened until the mid-1990s.[27]

The 1997 reform has supported job creation...

Against this background, the previous survey considered the 1997 labour market reform as a step in the right direction to redress labour market distortions related to the high level of EPL and reduce the high level of structural unemployment.

- A new permanent contract with lower firing costs was introduced for the recruitment of those most exposed to unemployment or those with a weak employment record (youth, workers above 45, long-term unemployed), supported by cuts in social security contributions during two years (between 20 and 60 per cent).
- The possibility of justified individual dismissals (which carry lower severance payments[28]) was extended from disciplinary reasons to *economic* reasons. However, the reform did not work effectively, since tribunals, who rule on most individual dismissals, continued to declare most of them as unjustified.
- An agreement was reached by the social partners aimed at avoiding renegotiations of wage settlements at different bargaining levels.

As a result of these changes, the overall level of EPL has been reduced throughout the 1990s, and is converging to the levels of Germany or France, but still remains above those of countries with more deregulated labour markets and lower rates of unemployment (Table 10). Furthermore, a very large majority of permanent workers are still under the old, more protective, type of contract, which is not reflected in the indices of the table.[29]

The introduction of a new permanent contract with reduced severance payments and social security contributions has supported the remarkable labour market performance since 1997. The unemployment rate dropped by 5.9 percentage points in little more than two years, to 15.5 per cent in the third quarter of 1999, and the number of permanent contracts has increased significantly. In 1998,

Table 10. **Strictness of EPL by international comparison: qualitative indices**[1]

	Regular employment		Temporary employment		Collective dismissals	Overall indicator	
	Late 1980s	Late 1990s	Late 1980s	Late 1990s	Late 1990s	Late 1980s	Late 1990s
France	2.3	2.3	3.1	3.6	2.1	2.7	3
Germany	2.7	2.8	3.8	2.3	3.1	3.2	2.5
United Kingdom	0.8	0.8	0.3	0.3	2.9	0.5	0.5
Italy	2.8	2.8	5.4	3.8	4.1	4.1	3.3
Portugal	4.8	4.3	3.4	3	3.6	4.1	3.7
Spain	**3.9**	**2.6**	**3.5**	**3.5**	**3.1**	**3.7**	**3.1**
Canada	0.9	0.9	0.3	0.3	3.4	0.6	0.6
United States	0.2	0.2	0.3	0.3	2.9	0.2	0.2

1. The index ranges from 0 to 6, with higher values representing stricter regulations. It corresponds to a subjective evaluation of a disaggregated set of indicators, so it must be interpreted with care. For Spain, the index does not take into account the stricter level of EPL for workers under the old permanent contract.
Source: OECD (1999). *Employment Outlook.*

Figure 11. **New permanent contracts: level and composition**

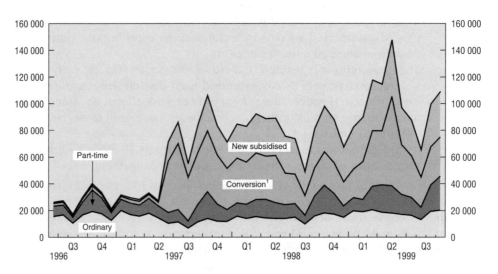

1. Temporary contracts converted into new, subsidised, permanent contracts.
Source: Ministry of Labour and Social Affairs, National Institute of Employment (INEM).

971 000 permanent contracts were signed, of which two-thirds were subsidised. Among subsidised permanent contracts signed in 1998, half were new ones and half were previously fixed-term contracts converted into permanent contracts (Figure 11). However, the share of wage earners under temporary contracts has remained at around 33 per cent since the end of 1997, an extremely high level by international comparison. Constraints on permanent hiring in the public sector have led to a significant rise of public employment on fixed-term contracts.

Since the reform was implemented, cuts in social security contributions have been extended and the targeting has been modified twice. In May 1999 (when the incentives were supposed to expire), reduced rates were prolonged for a third year to the new contracts signed since 1997, and the regime was extended up to January 2000 with lower subsidies for all categories (of between 25 and 50 per cent, depending on the targeted group), introducing a 5 percentage point differential in favour of female workers. While supporting employment creation, the reform had an annual gross budgetary cost of around 0.3 per cent of GDP in 1998 and 1999. By targeting a wide range of workers (including all young workers), it has subsidised jobs that would have probably been created in any case, incurring a dead-weight loss. At the same time, contribution rates have been increased by 0.5 to 1.5 per cent for temporary contracts, in order to penalise their use. As from 2000, incentives will be extended and re-designed again, increasing them for those groups of workers for which permanent employment was not rising much (long-term unemployed and old workers) and reducing them for the young. Conversions of former temporary into new permanent contracts will no longer be subsidised. As a general measure, a small reduction in unemployment insurance contributions (of 0.25 percentage points) has been introduced for all permanent contracts, new and old.

The co-existence of many types of contracts with different incentives tends to perpetuate labour market segmentation and might entail displacement effects. To minimise distortions, the existing incentives for permanent contracts should be further streamlined, with a view to improving their consistency with other regulations (e.g. the floors on social security contributions which raise the tax wedge on low-paid workers). Despite these side effects, the targeted measures introduced in 1997 have increased the employability of workers at the margin of the labour force, and have thereby raised the weight of "outsiders" in wage bargaining. The recent strong labour market performance tends to confirm that reduced levels of EPL and lower social security contributions support employment growth. More steps in the same direction, encompassing core worker groups, would help ensure the sustainability of the current high rate of employment growth. This would also reduce discrimination by sex and age and result in a more efficient allocation of human resources.

The system of wage bargaining has barely changed since the 1997 agreement between the social partners was adopted, and remains complicated. Some sectors, like banking and chemicals, apply national agreements on wages, which in some cases are re-negotiated at the firm level. In construction, there exists a cascading system by which national settlements are modified at the provincial level, and then possibly again at the firm level, resulting in higher wage inflation. In most other sectors, negotiations are conducted at the provincial level, though with some recommendations on wage increases from national organisations. The *cláusulas de descuelgue* – an opt-out possibility from provincial agreements in special situations (introduced in the 1994 reform) – are rarely used since the conditions allowing an opt-out (defined in collective agreements) are usually very restrictive. Moreover, their use may signal financial troubles of the companies concerned. The bargaining system has thus remained fairly inflexible. It should be changed to enhance companies' flexibility, as well as the geographic mobility of workers and take better account of differences in regional labour markets. National indicative wage agreements could be useful to maintain changes in unit labour costs in line with developments in the euro area.

... but further initiatives should be more comprehensive

Early in 1999, legislation concerning part-time work and temporary work agencies has been modified. To boost part-time employment, whose share in total employment is low in international comparison, the government has reduced social security contributions on new part-time permanent contracts. It has also equalised accrued rights of pensions to those on full-time contracts.[30] However, the new part-time contract is more rigid than the previous one in several respects. The maximum number of hours allowed was reduced from 99 per cent to 77 per cent of standard working time, including normal and complementary hours.[31] Moreover, the distribution of complementary hours during the year is not flexible, and it has to be communicated to the worker in advance. Some of these measures help the worker to organise in advance the working time, but also increase management costs, make planning difficult for firms, and may thus hinder part-time work. To enhance its effectiveness, the new part-time work regulation should be coupled with reforms to improve product market flexibility, especially by softening regulations concerning opening hours in retail trade.

The regulation of temporary work agencies has also been made more restrictive. The main objective of the reform is to regulate social rights of these workers, which were not well defined and were in general lower than those of workers with similar qualifications in the companies to which they are ceded. The new regulation obliges firms to pay them the same wage as for the incumbent workers of the same category in the work place, despite discrepancies in human capital acquired on the job. Their social security contributions have been raised by 1.5 percentage points (against a rise of only 0.5 per cent for normal temporary contracts), thus raising labour costs.

Unemployment benefits will be extended in 2000 for the long-term unemployed older than 45 years with children if their standard unemployment benefits have already expired. The measure will affect 50 000 individuals (around 4 per cent of the unemployed) and will consist of a monthly payment of ESP 53 000 during six months, conditional on job search in the previous three months. Although the budgetary cost of this measure is not very high (it is estimated at ESP 50 billion, or less than 0.1 per cent of GDP) and it is narrowly targeted, it may weaken incentives for active job search for other old unemployed workers who will be eligible for this program when their current subsidies will expire.[32]

Active labour market policies (ALMP) usually help groups of workers with greater difficulties to enter the labour market. Experience from other countries indicates that a good design of such measures is key for their success, given the risk of high dead-weight losses in some cases (for instance, in the case of direct subsidies or public employment programmes). In Spain, the Employment Plan for 1999 dedicates ESP 505 billion for ALMP, or roughly 0.7 per cent of GDP.[33] These funds are spread over various types of programmes, and are managed by different bodies. Unfortunately, there is no systematic information about their effectiveness (Sáez, 1997), and no detailed analysis exists that compares the relative success of different policies. A careful study that follows a sample of workers that are included in these programs would be needed to evaluate their usefulness.

Labour market measures have also been implemented at the regional level. The Catalan government has offered subsidies to new permanent contracts for prime age male workers (who are excluded from such incentives since the 1997 reform). At the same time, most Autonomous Communities (except Asturias, Baleares, Canarias and Murcia) have implemented various incentives that promote general reductions in hours worked in the private sector. In Andalucía, Cataluña and Galicia, social security contributions are now subsidised for those firms that apply the 35-hour week, and similar measures are being discussed in other regions. In addition, in Andalucía, Extremadura, Navarra and La Rioja, civil servants will work 35 hours a week as from 2000.[34] Such measures are likely to be detrimental to employment creation, since they reduce productivity without a corresponding reduction in labour cost, thus increasing unit labour costs. Cutting social security contributions to support a shorter working week would be probably only a partial offset to higher unit labour costs. Even if some employment is created in the short run it will be at a high budgetary cost for these governments.

While the 1997 reform has already shown positive effects, it remains incomplete in certain respects. More comprehensive reforms of employment protection legislation, encompassing core worker groups, would help consolidate the current employment gains and prevent discrimination by sex and age that may result in a less efficient allocation of labour. Alleviation of pressures on labour cost due to high social security contributions should be broader, while EPL for core workers should be reduced further. Because labour market institutions interact, the existence of a distortion can worsen the impact of other distortions. Policies to reform institutions should be comprehensive, as policy measures are often complementary and mutually reinforcing.

Comprehensive reforms are also needed in other areas. High and persistent discrepancies in unemployment across regions, for instance, are due to the low geographic mobility of labour.[35] In Spain unemployment is significantly higher in lower per capita income regions – as measured by the discrepancy of per capita GDP to the national average (Figure 12, first panel). This pattern of regional unemployment might result from lower demand for labour in low-productivity/less-developed regions leading to higher unemployment, as the lack of real wage differentials with high employment regions prevents worker mobility from removing the resulting imbalances in local labour markets. The lack of correlation between unemployment and regional wages (discrepancies with the national average adjusted for differences in standards of living) provides some supportive evidence on this. In fact, wage differentials – adjusted for differences in per capita income across regions – tend to be slightly *positively* correlated with regional unemployment (Figure 12, second panel).[36]

Figure 12.   **Unemployment, per capita income and wages across regions**
Per cent

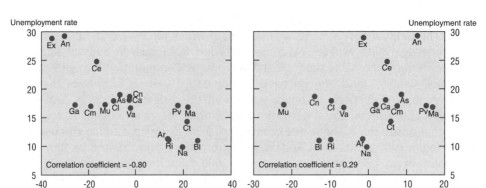

Note: An: Andalucía, Ar: Aragón, As: Asturias: Bl: Baleares, Cn: Canarias, Ca: Cantabria, Cm: Castilla-La Mancha,
Cl: Castilla y León, Ct: Cataluña, Va: Comunidad Valenciana, Ex: Extremadura, Ga: Galicia, Ma: Madrid, Mu: Murcia,
Na: Navarra, pv: País Vasco, Ri: Rioja (La), Ce: Ceuta y Melilla.
1.   Difference in per capita GDP to the national average.
2.   Difference to the national average adjusted for differences in standard of living, see footnote in text.
Source: INE and Encuesta de Salarios en la Industria y los Servicios, Base 1995 for GDP, 1998 for unemployment
and wages.

Several factors that hinder labour mobility are examined in various parts of the survey in connection with the functioning of goods markets and the structure of incentives embedded in the tax system. Among the more important factors is the underdevelopment of the market for rental housing, owing to restrictive regulations on the length of rental contracts, to high home prices and rentals (because of restricted urban land supply – see below), and to extensive home ownership. In turn, home ownership has been supported by tax preferences granted to owner-occupied housing in the personal income tax, which have been reduced but remain generous (see Chapter III). The inadequate structure of wage bargaining, which does not properly reflect relative slack in local labour markets, also impedes labour mobility. Weak incentives for job search arise, moreover, from unemployment benefits. Unemployment benefits – which are not very high in international comparison – are added to high severance payments provided by EPL, which are largely tax-exempt. Compensating the unemployed for the job loss by taking into account severance payments could enhance active job search. Incentives for regional mobility of labour are also weakened by the existence of income support programmes for seasonally unemployed farm workers, the most important of which is the *"Plan de Empleo Rural"* in Andalucía and Extremadura – the two regions with the highest rates of unemployment. Restricting the very loose eligibility conditions for these programmes and reducing the level of out-of-work assistance provided would raise the incentives of workers in these regions to search for jobs. Improved matching of workers and of employment opportunities could reduce the structural rate of unemployment.

Product markets

Subsidies could be lowered

Public support to industry has increased

In the mid-1990s, public support to manufacturing was below the EU average but it has been trending upwards and currently lies slightly above it (Figure 13, panel A). Up to 1993, sectoral public support programmes were largely used as a tool for restructuring shipyards, and the steel, coal mining, and defence-related industries, though the adjustment has been slow. The launch of the European Single Market called for a change in the pattern of public support to industry, to enforce cross-country discipline and prevent distortions in competition. This change in policy involved a shift from sector and product-specific support towards aid granted through horizontal policy programmes. In Spain, a significant shift has occurred mainly in the area of support to R&D, whose share in State aid to industry rose by more than 50 per cent between 1993 and 1997 (Figure 13, panel B). This reflects the concern of successive governments that Spain is lagging in R&D activities and innovation. Support to SMEs is a further key concern of horizontal programmes, with a share in the total which is broadly equivalent to that of R&D. Finally, though on a downward trend, almost one-third of ongoing programmes focused on regional development.[37]

Public support programmes to industry could distort product market competition. To minimise such risks, aid to industry should not be delivered in an *ad hoc* manner, outside horizontal programmes. In Spain, despite the commitment to increase support coverage under horizontal goals, the share of public aid to industry delivered under sector-specific objectives has increased between 1993 and 1997 (Figure 13, panel B). Moreover, spending under the heading of regional development aims mainly at promoting industrial investment in selected regions. It has become a main source of public support to some manufacturing industries with a strong regional concentration. In fact, about three-quarters of the labour force in declining industries (*e.g.* shipyards, steel and aluminium production) are concentrated in the northern regions of Spain. In addition, certain sectors like aeronautics and microelectronics are the main beneficiaries of the technology-specific slice of R&D support. Therefore, aside from restraining public support to industry, programmes should have a clear focus on horizontal objectives.

Figure 13. **Subsidies to industry and public services**

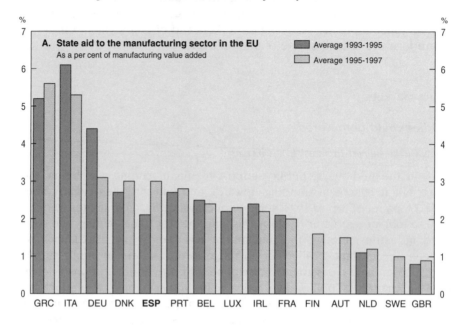

A. **State aid to the manufacturing sector in the EU**
As a per cent of manufacturing value added

- Average 1993-1995
- Average 1995-1997

GRC ITA DEU DNK **ESP** PRT BEL LUX IRL FRA FIN AUT NLD SWE GBR

B. **Breakdown of public support to industry and transport**

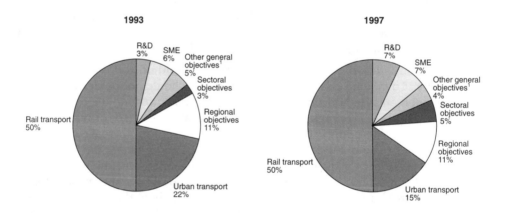

1993

R&D 3%
SME 6%
Other general objectives[1] 5%
Sectoral objectives 3%
Regional objectives 11%
Rail transport 50%
Urban transport 22%

1997

R&D 7%
SME 7%
Other general objectives[1] 4%
Sectoral objectives 5%
Regional objectives 11%
Rail transport 50%
Urban transport 15%

1. Including environmental, trade, energy saving and other objectives.
Source: European Commission and Ministry of Economy and Finance.

Support to public services needs further downsizing

Public support to the transport sector is sizeable and burdens the budget.[38] In 1997, State transfers to RENFE, the public railway company, and to urban transport companies in Madrid and Barcelona were almost twice as high as support granted to industry (Figure 13, panel B). Transfers to RENFE alone (including both current and capital transfers) amounted to 0.5 per cent of GDP. Though the public service character of rail and urban transport – as well as the resulting positive externalities – may warrant a certain degree of subsidisation, progress should be made to reduce operating costs.

RENFE's difficulties stem from declining rail transport demand (despite a recent increase in the number of passengers) and low passenger and freight rates, which have depressed earnings to barely half of operating costs and have forced the company to delay investments in infrastructure maintenance.[39] The separation of building and management of rail infrastructure – granted, as from 1997, to a new public entity, *Gestor de Infraestructuras Ferroviarias* (GIF) – from rail transport services will remedy this problem. The ongoing programme of infrastructure modernisation could, in the long run, restore the attractiveness of rail transport compared with road and air transport. Nevertheless, to reduce operation costs in the short run, steps should be taken to rationalise the network, possibly by decentralising management of secondary lines to the regions – following, for instance, the example of Germany. Costs could also be reduced by franchising parts of rail operations and by raising competition in other parts of the market (for instance, international and high-speed services). Setting up a regulatory body for rail transport would help ensure greater competition among rail operators. Nevertheless, to put RENFE on an equal footing with potential competitors, a sharing arrangement would need to be found for the sunk-cost part of its debt (the total amount of which is 1.2 per cent of GDP). Franchising might also help reduce the operational deficit of urban transport companies in Madrid and Barcelona. The privatisation in March 1999 of the inter-city bus company E*natcar* is a step in the right direction and could be implemented also in urban transport. It might be coupled, if needed, with a subsidy scheme. A wider assessment of transport pricing may also help: for instance, freight road haulage prices are below their marginal social cost in most countries (including their environment and congestion costs, among others). Raising them via higher taxes would increase the attractiveness of rail services.

Other public service enterprises that keep absorbing sizeable amounts of transfers are the postal service (*Correos y Telégrafos*) and the public broadcasting and TV operator RTVE. In 1998, transfers to these two public entities amounted to ESP 34.7 billion and ESP 11 billion respectively – which together nearly match the amount of aid granted to industrial R&D activities. Recent steps to update the postal services' regulatory framework – in accordance with the EU's liberalisation agenda – include the Universal Postal Service Law enacted in July 1998. To enhance transparency, the new framework has transformed *Correos y Telégrafos* into a public corporation, and has liberalised a part of postal services, while seeking to guarantee basic nation-wide services at affordable prices. Despite subsidies, RTVE's projected losses in 1999 amount to ESP 172 billion (0.2 per cent of GDP), while its outstanding debt should reach 0.9 per cent of GDP. To the extent that maintaining the public service in broadcasting is deemed necessary, revenue enhancing through user fees should be envisaged, as advertising revenue is – apart from State subsidies – currently RTVE's only source of receipts. Splitting the company's operations (radio, TV) to enhance cost-benefit transparency could also be envisaged.

Ample support to agriculture

Although Spanish agricultural exports have greatly benefited from the accession to the European Union, the sector's share in GDP has shrunk to 4 per cent in 1998 (against 5.6 per cent in 1986), while 40 per cent of agricultural jobs (around 700 000) have been lost. As in other EU countries, agriculture benefits from substantial support. In 1997, overall budgetary transfers amounted to ESP 941.8 billion[40] – nearly 27 per cent of the sector's value added (1.1 per cent of GDP). Almost 80 per cent of total budgetary transfers come in the form of payments via the EU's Common Agricultural Policy transfer schemes (FEOGA-Guarantee).[41] Subsidisation of private investment in agriculture amounts to nearly 8 per cent of total transfers, the rest covering restructuring programmes, rural development and other structural measures accompanying the CAP. Most of the budgetary support goes to producers of cereals (25 per cent), olive oil (20 per cent), oilseeds, beef and dairy products. The reform of the EU olive oil support scheme agreed in 1998 has particular significance as Spain is the world's largest producer. Spain was granted a National Guaranteed Quantity of 43 per cent of the EU's total production.

The FEGA (*Fondo Español de Garantía Agraria*) and the regional governments, following the CAP's general criteria, determine the national distribution of the transfers. In 1997, the regions channelled 72 per cent of total transfers to agriculture and fisheries. The distribution scheme tends to favour those areas with better performance within each sub-sector and to discourage low-productivity producers – aid is likely to benefit mostly rich farmers, because subsidies are still largely output based. Nevertheless, the government is considering to restrict the amount of aid provided to high income farmers (those with incomes exceeding ESP 3.3 million). Such a measure, like the distribution of subsidies, would have to be negotiated between the Ministry of Agriculture, autonomous communities and farmers' associations. Given the domestic leeway in the subsidy distribution provided by the EU guidelines, the whole process would benefit from more transparency and a clearer set of guidelines. Budgetary transfers from the CAP are

Figure 14. **National expenditures on agriculture in EU countries**
As a per cent of the GDP in agriculture[1]

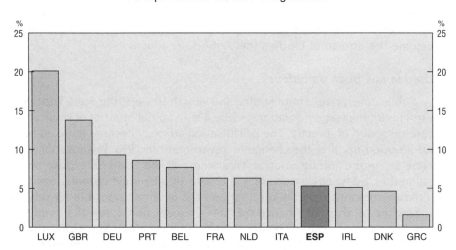

1. Average 1995-98 or latest available year,
Source: OECD, *National Accounts* and *Agricultural Policies in OECD Countries.*

complemented by national support programmes, which in 1995-98 amounted on average to 5 per cent of value added in agriculture (that is, nearly 20 per cent of total payments to the sector): this is at the lower range of EU countries national budgetary support to agriculture (Figure 14). National programmes mainly aim at the restructuring of production. A case in point is the two-year programme launched in 1998 to encourage non-competitive milk producers to cease production. Owing to the small size of dairy farms, half of them are considered as too small to achieve the standards set by the EU milk hygiene regulation. The authorities' initiatives included a milk-quota buying-up programme combined with an early retirement scheme.

Spanish producers have sought to strengthen their competitive position by improving quality and marketing especially of olive oil and wine. In contrast, cereal producers and cattle farmers have faced increasing pressure from imports. However, despite improved efficiency as a result of greater exposure of Spanish agriculture to foreign competition, yields are still below those in many other EU countries. Poor soil and uneven distribution of water, together with the small size of farms in some parts of the country account for low crop yields. In the north (especially in Galicia) most farms are inefficiently small, while in the south (particularly in Andalucía) estates are vast but sometimes neglected. A more rapid rise in agricultural productivity will be needed to prevent a further shrinking of the sector, as income support to agriculture could decline. The recent reform of agricultural policies within Agenda 2000 for the 2000-06 period will freeze the aid in nominal terms for the whole EU, while a further downsizing of support could be the result of EU enlargement. In anticipation of these trends, the national part of transfers to agriculture would need to provide adequate restructuring incentives to overcome the structural hurdles that impede productivity.

Privatisation has been ambitious

Public enterprise reform started in 1985. Until 1995, the State kept majority control in the biggest corporations, while a substantial number of small companies were disposed of directly. The privatisation strategy became more ambitious and was stepped up after the change in government in 1996. Privatisation guidelines were set in the "Modernisation Programme of the State Enterprise Sector", which aimed at a 5-year restructuring and sale of all public corporations in the State holding company's portfolio (SEPI) and the agent responsible for privatisation withing the Ministry of Finance (SEPPA) – except from a few that implement public policy (in rail transport, postal service, broadcasting). Major privatisations included *Endesa* in electricity, *Telefónica* and *Retevisión* in telecommunications, *Argentaria* in banking, *Aceralia* in steel, *Inespal* in aluminium and *Tabacalera* in tobacco (Table A1). Average annual privatisation proceeds in 1996-98 amounted to 1.6 per cent of GDP, three times as high as in 1993-95, placing Spain among the countries with the highest privatisation receipts in the OECD (Table 11). Privatisation was backed by strong local investor demand, leading to sizeable shareholdings of retail investors.

Table 11.   **Receipts from privatisation**

As a per cent of GDP

	1993-95[1]	1996-98[1]
Portugal	1.4	3.9
Hungary	5.2	2.5
Spain	**0.5**	**1.6**
Greece	0.0	1.6
Italy	0.5	1.4
Poland	0.4	1.2
Czech Republic	1.7	1.2
Finland	0.6	1.0
Austria	0.3	1.0
France	0.6	0.6
Belgium	0.6	0.6
Mexico	0.3	0.3
Netherlands	0.8	0.2
Japan	0.2	0.1

1.   Annual average.
Source: National Statistics and OECD Secretariat.

After the June 1998 sale of the remaining 30 per cent stake in Endesa, the privatisation programme was temporarily halted owing to the financial turmoil in the second half of 1998. Nevertheless, the SEPI announced in December 1998 that the programme was to resume and to be completed in 1999, with the sale of remaining stakes in six more companies. Most important of them are: Ence, a pulp and paper producer; Santa Bárbara, a defence group; and Iberia, the national air carrier. It is noteworthy that the national carrier, which made losses until 1995, improved its performance significantly and posted a profit of € 320 million in 1998.

Competition policy is being reformed

Because traditional macroeconomic tools have limited power at the national level in the context of monetary union, the Spanish authorities consider that strengthening competition is an important tool to contain inflation differentials vis-à-vis its European partners. In April 1999, the government established the compulsory notification of merger plans, if the new firm is to control 25 per cent or more of a given market or its turnover is higher than ESP 40 billion.[42] Besides, competition authorities face the challenge derived from cross-participations of financial institutions in network industries, stemming from the consolidation process in the banking industry. The government has recently proposed reforms to the Competition Law of 1989 (Box 4) in an attempt to

---

Box 4. **The proposed reform of the 1989 Competition Law**

In June 1999, the government proposed a reform of the Competition Law aimed at increasing the powers and resources of competition bodies. Main features of the draft law include:

- An increase in the Tribunal's financial and staff resources. The proposal includes adding staff to the Tribunal and granting it with the receipts of a new fee, paid by the companies concerned for the analysis of merger cases (of between ESP 500 000 and ESP 2 million, depending on the size of the merger). The Tribunal will also be able to apply the principle of "selective intervention", i.e. to decide not to follow cases of little practical relevance in order to concentrate on key cases.
- The review on the impact of public subsidies on competition. The Tribunal will be able to conduct an independent analysis, and advise the government on subsidy programmes.
- Reinforcing the Tribunal's capacity to impose sanctions for anti-competitive practices and accelerating the decision process. This includes authorising fines for continued violations, of from ESP 10 000 to ESP 500 000 per day, increasing other powers of investigation, and reducing the maximum time for proceedings from 18 to 12 months.

---

enhance the instruments available for competition surveillance. The changes aim at raising the effectiveness of the two main competition institutions: the *Servicio de Defensa de la Competencia*, which depends on the Ministry of Finance and carries out preparatory work; and the *Tribunal de Defensa de la Competencia*, an independent body that resolves matters, based on the Servicio's reports and on its own investigations. The proposed law would also give the Tribunal the capacity to advise the government on the criteria for providing subsidies. To further strengthen the regulatory framework of competition policy, Spain could consider combining the functions into a single independent competition authority with a clear mandate. Merging the Servicio and the Tribunal would imply a better use of staff resources and reduce decision delays.

Sectoral reform has progressed

Telecommunications

Spain has progressed rapidly towards the full liberalisation of the telecommunication sector over the past two years. *Retevisión* started competing with Telefónica as a second operator in basic telephony in January 1998, and has captured a sizeable market share. Others have also started operating since December 1998 when the market was opened (*Lince, Jazztel* and *British Telecom*). Price competition has intensified and long-distance prices have dropped, although local tariffs and monthly subscriber charges have risen as prices have been re-balanced to better reflect costs. In April and October 1999, the government announced new measures to enhance competition. They include: the introduction of a calendar to guarantee the preselection of the operator in long distance calls, further cuts in long distance, fixed-to-mobile and local tariffs combined with future increases of monthly subscriber charges, and the introduction of a price cap system based on a basket of services provided by *Telefónica* by August 2000. In mobile telecommunications, a fourth license is to be awarded shortly and portability of numbers will be introduced by July 2000. Several of the new operators have links to international telecommunications giants, which ensures the implementation of state-of-the-art technologies. Customer choice and quality are thus improving. The sectoral regulator (*Comisión del Mercado de las Telecomunicaciones*) is well empowered and has obtained some early successes, particularly with regard to significantly bringing down *Telefónica's* interconnection prices towards the lowest in the EU. However, several problems in the liberalisation process have been identified (OECD, 1999c). The lack of a proper accounting separation requirement for the incumbent makes the detection of anticompetitive cross-subsidisation difficult and could deter potential new entrants. In the future, interconnection prices should be based explicitly on long-run incremental costs, rather than on the current concept of "real cost", which is ambiguous. Moreover, the conditions attached to licenses have been very demanding and have translated into high start-up costs for new companies. Moreover, *Telefónica* should be required to divest its cable television operations, in order to stimulate competition in telephone services in the local market from other cable operators.

Electricity

Spain has deregulated the electricity sector further and more quickly than most other EU countries. The Spanish electricity reform law, passed in December 1997, has created a wholesale market, introduced choice for the largest electricity customers and cut prices for those remaining under regulated tariffs. Amendments in December 1998 and April 1999 widened the choice for medium-sized consumers, further cut regulated prices, and encouraged greater activity in the wholesale market by lowering access tariffs. However, though electricity prices have dropped by about 11 per cent in nominal terms since 1996, domestic prices before tax are still among the highest in the OECD. The government has also sold all its shares in the country's largest utility, Endesa, and plans to dispose of its majority shareholding in Red Eléctrica, the national transmission company.[43] By limiting electricity companies' participation into Red Eléctrica's capital to 40 per cent, the government has reinforced provisions aiming at the independence between electricity producers and distributors.

To reap the full benefits of this deregulation process, the government should address some pending issues. These are laid out in detail in the 1999 OECD Report on Regulatory Reform in Electricity which is forthcoming. First, the market is still highly concentrated, with two incumbent companies capturing 80 per cent of the market, and little competition from imports exists.[44] Furthermore, the two largest generating companies have established strategic links with oil and gas companies, which are *de facto* an oligopoly and a monopoly, respectively. Privileged access to the upstream sectors could further benefit the incumbents. Second, there are a number of energy policy costs that small consumers have to pay for through higher electricity prices.[45] Third, differentiated regulated prices, which entail some cross-subsidisation from captive to large consumers, further hinder competition. Specifically, regulated prices for large consumers have been set below costs. Fourth, the sectoral regulator (Comisión Nacional del Sistema Eléctrico, CNSE) has an advisory and mediation role but lacks legal authority. The gradual transfer of some regulatory powers from the Industry Ministry would improve transparency and boost confidence in the independence of energy-related decisions, thus promoting new entrance in the generation market. International experience suggests various options to enhance competition in generation: restricting the construction of new capacity by dominant companies so as to allow an increase in the market share of others, or requiring them to lease some of their capacity. As a last resort, major players could be broken up into smaller production units.

Hydrocarbons

Progress in the deregulation of the gas sector, which is currently dominated by a *de facto* integrated monopoly (*Gas Natural*), is essential. It would also be key to improving the electricity sector's future performance since gas is bound to become a critical input to power generation. Recent steps to liberalise the gas sector in Spain have been more ambitious than in many other EU countries. The 1998 Hydrocarbon law has liberalised gas supply to large consumers and power generators, and provided third party access to pipelines and LNG terminals. In April 1999, the government decided to further liberalise the gas sector. As part of the April 1999 anti-inflationary package, the government announced cuts in natural gas tariffs for households.[46] Amendments to the 1998 Hydrocarbon law also lowered the transition period for full price liberalisation to 10 years and the consumption threshold to benefit from the liberalised segment of the market from 20 to 10 million cubic meters annually (and to 5 million in January 2000). In October 1999, the government also granted temporary authorisations for the entrance of new firms in the gas distribution sector. However, *Gas natural* will likely remain the dominant supplier for some time because its existing long-term supply contracts fill nearly all the existing pipeline capacity. In order to enhance competition in the sector, some measures should be considered. These include: increasing the degree of management independence between distribution and transport activities which are currently controlled by *Gas Natural*, owner of ENAGAS which operates the high pressure transmission system; cutting third party access tariffs to the transport system and the period of exclusive distribution in a given geographical area (currently 10 years); and the encouragement of new conveyance, transformation and storage facilities. In the oil sector, the government announced in October 1999 some measures to enhance competition at the retail level, thus reducing inflation pressures. They include: the obligation to advertise gasoline prices on highways and petrol stations, and a change in the nature of concession contracts between petrol stations an wholesalers.[47] Nevertheless, restrictive regulations on the supply of land by local authorities could still limit the opening of new petrol stations and thus inhibit competition, and licensing regulations to distribute oil products in supermarkets need to be streamlined. Measures to promote the independence of the oil transport and storage system are also needed. These two activities are in fact controlled by the three main players in the refining market through their joint ownership of *Compañía Logística de Hidrocarburos* (CLH) which owns 95 per cent of the storage capacity, and transports about 95 per cent of fuels.

Water

Water is a scarce resource but prices in Spain are low and differentiated by economic activity, thus creating distortions in its allocation. Consumption is almost free and particularly high in agriculture, which accounts for around 80 per cent of total demand. Water supply for urban consumption is regulated by local authorities, and there is a wide variety of economic regimes and pricing systems. Some local governments manage a local public enterprise, while others tender concessions to private companies. Prices vary across municipal areas from ESP 60 per cubic meter in Galicia to ESP 200 in Cataluña. Though these differences reflect the relative scarcity of water resources, prices are so low that they do not even cover distribution costs. The pricing system should become more rational and competition in water resource management could be introduced by periodically auctioning public concessions. At the end of 1998, the government published a white paper that outlines the future *Plan Hidrológico Nacional*. It envisages large transfers of water across some regions, since the natural distribution of water resources in Spain is quite unbalanced (against the East and South-East of the country). The plan requires payment for this water supply, thus introducing at least a partial incentive to save water. The investment for the transport of water is very costly, however. Priority should thus be given to other measures to save water. The reform of the 1985 Water Law includes such measures. It led to the implementation of a market for water for some users (but not for electricity companies) and made water metering compulsory for all consumers, with the aim to improve water pricing. Introducing a market of property rights for water resources would improve incentives to control leaks in water distribution, which are reported to be very large. However, the reform does not address the problem of excessive consumption, since it does not modify the original permit system for water use, which implies that the average price of water is low for those who obtain a permit.

Land reform

The Spanish housing market is characterised by a high proportion of home ownership and a rigid supply of land. The lack of rental housing reduces labour mobility, and is the consequence of the length of rental contracts (five years) and a very favourable fiscal treatment of owner-occupied housing that reduces demand for rental housing (see Chapter III). A shortage in land supply has been one of the main reasons for the sharp increase of housing prices close to cyclical peaks. This lack of supply response reflects the fact that it takes municipalities a long time (up to five years) to provide a license to use land for construction. Moreover, they apply arbitrary criteria in providing licenses and land buyers have to cede a share of the land to the municipality for urban development purposes. This share was reduced from 15 per cent to 10 per cent in 1998. Local governments, who control most of the supply of urban land, are interested in keeping prices high, as land sales constitute an important share of municipal income. A reform of local governments' legislation that improves the flexibility of land supply by clearly determining which areas can be urbanised, and streamlines administrative procedures, is needed to improve the uses of soil.

It should go together with a comprehensive reform of local revenues that reduces the reliance on real estate taxes.

Retail shopping hours

Enhanced competition in retail trade would increase consumer choice and put downward pressure on retail prices. Extended *shop opening hours* would also raise employment opportunities, which should be boosted by the new part-time contract. The 1996 Trade Law and accompanying legislation gave the right to the regions to limit retail opening hours. Regional governments can since then restrict opening hours per week and the number of open Sundays per year, though not below a 72-hour threshold and 8 Sundays, respectively. Most regions have stuck to these limits, thus restricting opening time with respect to the previous situation of more liberal opening hours. However, by January 2001 a move to a complete liberalisation of opening hours is envisaged, conditional on an agreement between the central and regional governments. In addition to restrictions on opening hours, several *entry barriers* remain in different areas. According to the 1996 Trade Law, new hypermarkets need licensing of regional governments, which has been frequently denied. As for sale periods, the Trade Law limits them to twice a year, following a schedule that is determined by the regions. Administrative procedures required for business start-ups are heavy, despite some improvements over the past few years, and land use restrictions also create an entry barrier. In this respect, the extension of a new advisory service at the provincial level (*ventanilla única*) that aims at reducing the number of steps needed to open a new business should help in reducing the administrative burden. Some sectors are also affected by specific barriers. For instance, the establishment of new pharmacies is heavily restricted (*e.g.* minimum distance between them, or minimum number of inhabitants per pharmacy in a given area). Furthermore, *price regulations* remain, *e.g.* for books or pharmaceuticals. Discounting for school books is only allowed up to 12 per cent from the publisher's reference price.[48]

Financial markets

Banking consolidation has progressed and could raise new policy issues for prudential supervision

In Spain, as in other OECD countries, the process of banking consolidation has gained momentum in the 1990s (Figure 15, panel A). It was partly spurred by the prospect of the development of a more integrated banking industry in the euro area. Moreover, the development of new banking technology and distribution channels has underlined the excess capacity and fragmentation of most European banking systems, pointing to the need for consolidation to share costs

Figure 15. **Trends in the banking system**

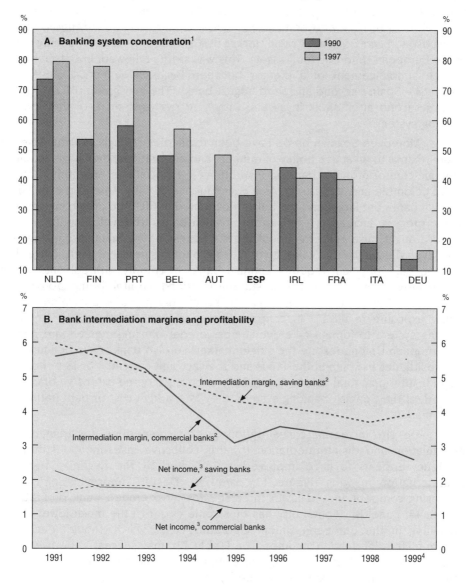

1. Concentration is defined as assets of the five largest credit institutions as a percentage of the total assets of domestic credit institutions.
2. Difference between lending and deposit rates for 1 to 3 year maturities.
3. As a per cent of average balance sheet total.
4. Third quarter.
Source: European Central Bank, Ministry of Economy and Finance, Bank of Spain and OECD, *Bank Profitability.*

and take advantage of scale economies. In Spain, consolidation has occurred among both commercial and savings banks (*Cajas de ahorro*). A sizeable merger occurred in April 1999, between B*anco de Santander* and B*anco Central Hispano* (BCH), giving rise to B*anco Santander Central Hispano* (BSCH), the 19th largest banking group in the European Union by total assets. This was swiftly followed, in October 1999, by the announcement of a merger between B*anco Bilbao Vizcaya* (BBV) and A*rgentaria* – Spain's second and third largest banks. The new group (BBVA) will be Spain's second after BSCH in assets, with a 10 per cent share of the Spanish banking system.[49]

Moreover, Spanish banks have been expanding strongly in Latin America where, thanks to an active policy of mergers and acquisitions, they have acquired strategic control of major banking institutions – especially in Argentina, Bolivia, Chile, Colombia and Venezuela. As a consequence of Latin American expansion, Spanish banks are larger and are better positioned in the euro-area bank consolidation process. Increasing exposure of Spanish banks to developments in Latin America might raise concerns about the soundness of the Spanish banking system, given the substantial volatility of these economies in recent years. Nevertheless the Bank of Spain requires Spanish banks to comply with solvency ratios significantly above international standards (tier-1 capital being above the EU norm).[50] This leads to a higher capitalisation that provides a cushion for the higher exposure to risks.[51] In contrast to the openness of the Latin American banking system to foreign take-overs, cross-border banking mergers are rare in the European Union, despite the single market. Foreign banks have begun to set up subsidiaries in Spain in the 1980s and they account currently for 13 per cent of credit institutions' total assets. Nevertheless, because of the extensive branching network of the Spanish banking system, they face a high cost in penetrating the retail market.

Despite increasing concentration, greater competition was triggered by deregulation and disintermediation towards collective investment institutions. Efficiency appears to have improved as indicated by the declining trend in intermediation margins (Figure 15, panel B). Despite improving efficiency, increasing competition and lower interest rates have eroded bank profitability (Figure 15, panel B). Profitability has thus come closer to the much lower levels prevailing in the European Union. Operating costs, which, though declining, remain high in international comparison (Table 12), may suggest a lower level of efficiency of Spanish banks.[52] High operating costs reflect the branch intensive character of Spanish banking. Measured by the number of bank branches relative to inhabitants, Spain turns out to be the most over-banked euro area country – though this may also partly reflect the focus of banks on the retail segment of the market and the low population density of the country. Moreover, in contrast to the consolidation in banking capacity that has occurred in some other European Union countries during the 1990s, branches and employment have both been

Table 12. **International comparison of bank profitability**

1997, as a per cent of average balance sheet total

	Spain		Austria	France	Germany	Italy	Netherlands	Portugal
	Commercial banks	Saving banks						
Net interest income	2.1	3.2	1.5	0.8	1.7	2.4	1.8	2.0
Non-interest income (net)	1.1	0.9	1.1	1.0	0.5	1.0	1.2	0.9
Gross income	3.2	4.1	2.7	1.8	2.3	3.4	3.0	2.9
Operating expenses	2.0	2.4	1.9	1.2	1.5	2.3	2.1	1.8
Net income	1.2	1.7	0.8	0.6	0.8	1.0	0.9	1.2
Provisions (net)	0.4	0.5	0.4	0.3	0.3	0.7	0.2	0.4
Profit before tax	0.8	1.2	0.4	0.3	0.5	0.3	0.7	0.8
Number of credit institutions' branches[1]	1.0[2]	..	0.6	0.4	0.6	0.4	0.4	0.4
(Difference between 1997 and 1990)	(0.1)[2]		(0.0)	(0.0)	(–0.1)	(0.1)	(–0.1)	(0.2)
Number of credit institutions' employees[1]	6.3[2]	..	9.4	6.9	9.2	6.0	7.2	6.0
(Difference between 1997 and 1990)	(0.1)[2]		(–0.4)	(–0.7)	(–1.9)	(0.1)	(–0.7)	(–0.2)

1. Per 1 000 inhabitants.
2. Commercial banks and saving banks.
Source: ECB, *Monthly Bulletin* and OECD, *Bank Profitability.*

expanding in Spain even in most recent years (Table 12).[53] The ongoing process of bank concentration is expected to eventually improve profitability by reducing capacity and operating costs through a rationalisation of banking networks. Nevertheless, the speed of this process could be slow in Spain due to the existing employment protection legislation.

Lower bank profitability may be of concern as it might induce banks to take more risks in lending and asset management. This could be of particular relevance in the current conjuncture, where the low level of interest rates and the rapid pace of economic growth may create the seeds for an unsustainable credit expansion. It is noteworthy that mortgage and consumer credit have been growing at a two-digit percentage rate for several years, and accounted in 1998 for 32 per cent of credit liabilities, against 19 per cent in 1991. Continued vigilance on the part of the supervisory authorities is therefore called for. In particular, asset price inflation in the housing market should be monitored, with a view to raising bank lending standards should collateral prices become inflated. This would limit the risks of an unsustainable credit expansion. A hardening of the required provisioning on lending (including real estate loans) is actually being considered. Moreover, despite the expected gains in efficiency, a process of bank concentration involves a substantial increase in the size of financial institutions that could potentially present dangers for the soundness of the banking system. If the increase in the size of institutions is perceived as favouring a "too-big-to-fail" attitude on the part of the authorities, monitoring incentives by depositors and owners of large institutions may weaken. The moral hazard problem resulting from such an implicit insurance on banking bailouts may induce banks to take more risks than otherwise, increasing thereby the likelihood of bank failures (Mishkin, 1999).

Vigilant prudential supervision, with special focus on the largest banking institutions, will be necessary to respond to such risks. The high capital standards of Spanish banks should not be considered as a sufficient safeguard, as traditional capital adequacy ratios may become of less relevance in a more complex financial environment where new instruments allow quick changes in positions. Enhanced assessment of risk management processes of individual institutions will become even more necessary to enforce an adequate level of banking supervision.[54] Enhanced co-ordination of banking supervision across euro area countries could also become necessary as a result of the increasing cross-border character of banking operations – especially in the wholesale segment of the market.

Market forces should be allowed to shape the structure of the banking system

Further progress in the rationalisation of the banking system would also need to embrace savings banks, which account currently for 37 per cent of total bank assets. Savings banks are credit institutions with a peculiar legal status: they are foundations attached to their own regions, with no equity capital and shareholders, whose profits partly fund regional projects of social interest (*obra social*). Autonomous communities, municipalities, local corporations, associations of employees and other founding members control savings banks through their membership in the governing bodies. Given their regional origins, savings banks are strongly anchored in the retail segment of local credit markets and they also capture a large part of the market for mortgage credit.[55] Partly reflecting this specialisation and also due to their expanding branch network, operating costs are significantly higher for savings banks than for commercial banks. Nevertheless, partly because of higher intermediation margins in the retail market segment, savings banks post a slightly better profitability than commercial banks (Table 12). Yet, savings banks' profitability might be eroded in the future, making restructuring more urgent, if, for instance, currently overgenerous tax incentives to

Figure 16. **The size of the securities markets**
Capitalisation as a per cent of GDP, end 1997

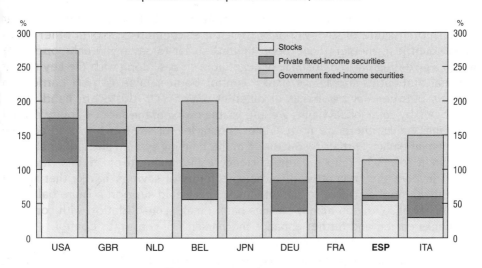

Source: BIS, Morgan Stanley and OECD.

eventually promote private sector issues. Moreover, the single currency area will increase the liquidity of the European capital markets, reducing the cost of funds and offer more opportunities for low-cost private issues of debt and equity. As a result, traditional bank borrowing can be expected to lose further ground to private debt issuance.

Against this background, to help private businesses – especially small and young, more risky, companies – to take advantage of the opportunities of expanding securities markets, the Spanish authorities have introduced a series of supportive financial regulations. The regulatory framework of capital markets seems now to broadly fit the financing requirements of the economy, though the need for further reform should be assessed in the light of the business response to the newly created opportunities. The most important capital market reform measures included:

– easing the requirements a firm needs to fulfil to be listed on a stock exchange (as from June 1997). More specifically, the CNMV can waive the profitability requirement during the two to five years prior to the listing at a stock exchange, if future profitability is likely – affecting most importantly privatisations, mergers and spin-offs;

housing were to be phased out (see chapter on options for reformin system), given their extensive mortgage credit lending.

Despite the absence of regulatory restrictions, but reflecting the ownership structure of savings banks (which is encountered also in otl pean countries), mergers have been limited so far to savings banks within a given region. The absence of negotiable shares, along with the k regional authorities in savings banks' control bodies, raise de facto be mergers between savings banks of different regions. On the other har take-overs by commercial banks are impossible owing to the lack of equit of savings banks, there are no regulatory obstacles for savings banks to commercial banks. Further restructuring of the banking system should be by market forces to reap greater efficiency gains. Main steps in this would involve the promotion of ownership forms of savings banks tha make them more sensitive to market forces. This would support a more b pattern of consolidation among savings banks; make consolidation with c cial banks easier; and further enhance mechanisms of corporate control.

Reforms to facilitate business access to capital markets

Capitalisation of the Spanish stock and government bond ma broadly in line with that of continental European countries (Figure 16) market turnover has been boosted by the massive privatisations carri recently, even though the structure of the market remains relatively unbal Stock market turnover is mostly concentrated in a few sectors (telecomm tions, banking, energy) and in some large firms, even though fees for adm operation of stocks and for complementary services provided by the CNMV sión Nacional del Mercado de Valores) and the markets are comparatively low.[56] over, private bond issues are rare, signalling a difficult access of private nesses to non-bank financing. The large public sector borrowing requireme to the mid 1990s, as well as the absence of a withholding tax on interest government bonds, may have crowded out the issuance of private bonds. induced distortions have been waived as from December 1998 by eliminatin withholding at source of the corporate tax on income from corporate bonds

Over the 1990s, capital market deepening has been supported by si cant disintermediation that has occurred as a result of declining bank dej interest rates. This has induced investors to seek improved risk/return comb tions by better diversifying their portfolios. Hence a growing share of housel savings has been ploughed into investment funds (benefiting up to 1998 k more favourable tax treatment), insurance companies and pension funds. A result, the relative size of Spanish investment funds' assets has surpassed euro area average.[57] The growing role of collective investment institutic by bringing a large number of small investors to the securities markets, n

- enabling companies listed at the stock exchange to issue preferred stock, redeemable shares, non-voting shares, and facilitating capital increases by reducing the time period to exercise the subscription right by former shareholders (as from 1998). This enlarged the range of assets available to investors and created securities that combine a level of risk intermediate between fixed-income securities and common stock;

- softening regulations of collective investment institutions (as from 1997). In particular, investment funds have been allowed to invest up to 10 per cent of their assets in unlisted securities (5 per cent in the case of money-market funds). Moreover, as from 1998, master-feeder funds, funds of funds and funds specialised in unlisted securities have been introduced, while mergers between funds have been allowed so as to benefit from economies of scale and reduced portfolio management fees;

- liberalising venture capital regulations by: i) defining venture capital in a very open way. Granting of the venture capital entity status involves temporal participation for at least 60 per cent of the company's assets in the capital of unlisted enterprises. However, venture capital entities are not allowed to invest more than 25 per cent of their assets in one company, or 35 per cent in the same company group; and ii) granting a favourable tax regime to venture capital companies by exempting from the corporate income tax 99 per cent of the capital gains obtained on assets held for at least 3 years (and up to 12 years). Nevertheless, to further promote reallocation of funds across young innovative companies, the minimum required holding period for the capital gains tax relief could be reduced further;

- facilitating securitisation and cession of assets, by extending to a broader spectrum of debt claims securitisation possibilities that were previously available only to mortgages. The new regulation concerns the activities of "asset substitution funds", which, subject to certain transparency and auditing conditions, can engage in purchases of a varied spectrum of both bank and non-bank assets (mortgages, credit card receivables, corporate promissory notes, commercial credit, tolls from highway concessions and other future claims). Securitisation of assets is particularly attractive for companies, since it helps restructure their balance sheets by transferring certain risks. It is also attractive for investors since it increases possibilities of portfolio selection and risk diversification. Enhancing credit institutions' possibilities to securitise their assets will provide them with more flexibility in risk management and hence could reduce the cost of credit especially to small enterprises. Thus, in an indirect way, enhanced securitisation would allow SMEs to reap some of the benefits from financial disintermediation.

Public sector issues

Pension reform needs to be taken up again

The pension system will become unsustainable in the medium term...

Measures implemented in July 1997 – following the October 1996 agreement between social partners based on the Toledo Pact – have generated savings so that the pay-as-you-go pension system will be broadly in balance in 1999.[58] Outlays and receipts currently represent around 9 per cent of GDP, which is low in international comparison. However, the viability of the pension system will come under increasing strain as a result of population ageing. The dependency ratio is projected to deteriorate significantly (Figure 17), with demographic developments in Spain less favourable than elsewhere due to the very low birth rate.[59] With such a high dependency ratio, the increase in social security contributions that would be called for to ensure the sustainability of the pay-as-you-go system could involve a substantial loss of output and jobs.[60] This would further undermine the sustainability of the system.

Apart from population ageing, pressures on the pension system also stem from its generosity in comparison with the pension systems in other OECD countries. Currently the replacement rate for 35 years of contribution is nearly 85 per cent of the final wage (and even higher for a relatively flat earnings profile), implying a considerably higher accumulation rate than in most other OECD countries. Despite its recent widening to 15 years, the pensions' base is still rather narrow compared with other OECD countries. In Germany or the United Kingdom, for instance, pension entitlements are based on contributions made during a person's entire working life.

Incentives to early retirement also impose a high cost on the social security system, since they imply a double cost (more benefits are paid, and less social security contributions are received). In Spain, one possibility is to retire early after age 60 for an individual that has worked for 35 years, with a reduction of 8 per cent in pension rights for each year of anticipation before age 65. This penalty is high compared to other countries. However, the high replacement ratio, combined with a front-loaded system to accumulate pension rights (with 50 per cent occurring within the first 15 years of contributions and 80 per cent in the first 25 years) imply that *de facto* incentives to early retirement are high. This is highlighted by the implicit average tax on continuing work beyond the age of 55, computed by the OECD Secretariat (Figure 18),[61] for which Spain stands slightly

Figure 17. **Elderly dependency ratios**[1]
Per cent

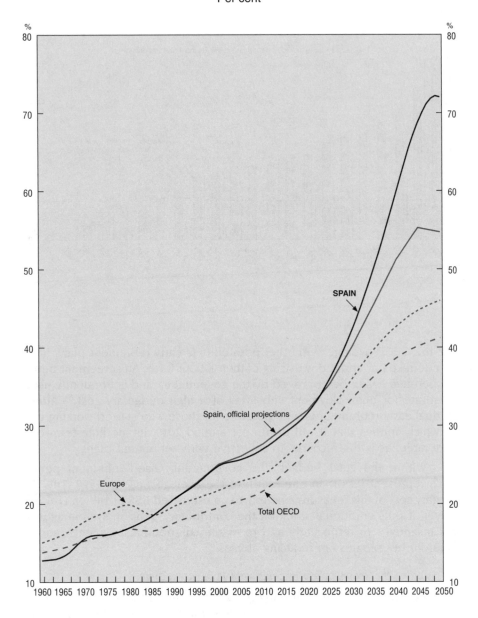

1. Population aged 65 and over as a per cent of working age population.
Source: United Nations and Ministry of Economy and Finance.

Figure 18. **Implicit average tax rate on continuing work from 55 to 64**
In per cent, 1995

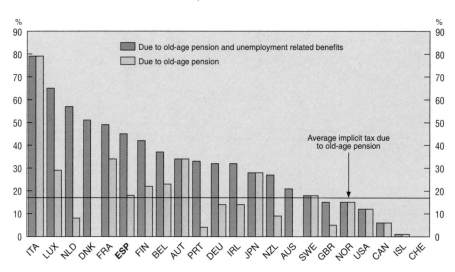

Source: OECD Secretariat.

above the OECD average.[62] Another possibility is early retirement plans in firms that undertake important downsizing of their labour force. An agreement between social partners has to be approved by the government, and is frequently used as a substitute for unemployment subsidies at a high budgetary cost.[63] Although individual early retirement is only possible for those who started working before 1967, which implies that it will disappear around 2010, its medium term cost is considerable, as is the recourse to collective early retirement plans.

Within the 2000 budget, the government raised minimum pensions – which represent less than one fourth of the average wage in 1999. The direct budgetary cost of this measure amounts to an estimated ESP 61 billion (Table 13). However, it puts additional strain on the contributory pension system as it reinforces incentives to retire early and to evade contribution payments, and thus calls for further progress in reducing abuses.[64]

... and the upcoming reform would need to be far-reaching

Far-reaching reform following the 2000 Round of the Toledo Pact discussions would provide an opportunity to prevent a further increase in labour taxation and ensure the sustainability of the pension system. As further increases in contributions or in income taxes to finance pensions could harm employment,

Table 13. **Minimum pension adjustment in 2000**

	Monthly pension in 1999 in pesetas[1]	Number of recipients (in thousands)	Increase in 2000 (%)	Increase in 2000 after adjustment for inflation (net budgetary cost of the measure)[2]
Old age and invalidity pensions				
For a pensioner older than 65, with a spouse	67 050	350	5.4	9.1
For a pensioner under 65, with a spouse	58 690	48	6.1	1.4
For a pensioner older than 65, single	56 990	908	5.3	19.3
For a pensioner under 65, single	49 735	60	6.0	1.4
Survivor pension				
Older than 65	56 990	679	5.3	14.4
Younger than 65	49 735	59	6.0	1.4
Younger than 60, with family responsibilities	45 480	12	16.0	1.0
Younger than 60, without family responsibilities	37 955	48	10.9	2.1
Non-contributory pensions				
One recipient	37 955	458	6.1	8.4
Old-age and invalidity mandatory insurance	40 750	326	4.0	2.7
Total	**52 812**	**2 944**	**5.5**	**61.3**

1. As budgeted for 1999.
2. The estimation discounts the 2.0 per cent official inflation projection incorporated in the 2000 budget and the compensation for above projected inflation in 1999. The monthly pension is paid 14 times a year (including two special installments in July and December).
Source: Official estimates.

especially of the low skilled, the renegotiation of the Toledo Pact should consider reducing the generosity of the pension system. The main options involve: a) Widening the pension base, possibly to working life contributions; b) Tightening eligibility conditions for early retirement and strengthening incentives to continue work by reducing front-loading of pension rights accrual; c) Lifting ceilings of contributions to reduce the regressivity of the current scheme; and d) Providing adequate incentives for older workers to continue work after the legal retirement age.

Pension reform would be more effective if carried out in a comprehensive way, in tandem with other labour market reforms. For example, if continuing work by older workers were to be encouraged, more flexible patterns of part-time work may be needed to accommodate the increasing participation of older workers. In addition, pension reform could be an opportunity to review regulations concerning immigrant workers' participation in the labour force. In Spain, migratory flows are currently subject to controls, up to an authorised annual quota of 30 000 non-EU workers. Yet, the immigrant population in Spain still represents a smaller share of the labour force compared with other EU countries (1 per cent, according to the 1991 census, against 6 per cent in France). According to estimates,[65] allowing an increase in immigration to an annual quota of 100 000 workers would improve the sustainability of the pay-as-you-go system by reducing its projected deficit in 2040 by around 2 per cent of GDP.

Moreover, the new round of the Toledo Pact discussions would provide an opportunity to make a transition to a mixed system combining pay-as-you-go and funding. The creation of a ESP 60 billion reserve fund in the 2000 budget is a step in this direction. This could also be achieved by allowing contributors to transfer part of their contributions to a privately run pension fund system. Workers who retire could thus receive pensions partly from the pay-as-you-go system and partly from the capitalisation of mandatory contributions to pension funds. Transition to a mixed system would substantially increase social security imbalances over the medium term, as the system would lack part of the resources needed to cover currently retiring workers. These costs (involving basically a higher medium term tax effort) would have to be balanced against the long-run benefits stemming from a less severe adjustment in the tax/benefit parameters of the pay-as-you-go system. In addition, financial deepening resulting from the accumulation of private pension savings could have positive side effects on economic efficiency and growth. Finally, partial transition to a capitalisation system would strengthen individual responsibility in the management of the retirement decision and would redress the incentives for early retirement embedded in the structure of the current system.

Health care reform has been progressing slowly

Health care spending does not deviate significantly from that of other OECD countries, taking into account per capita income differences, but has risen steeply since the late 1980s. Furthermore, despite the ample supply of health services (the number of doctors and pharmacists per inhabitant largely surpasses the OECD average, see Table 14), long waiting lists for public hospitals and public health centres still exist. Moreover, preventive care is underdeveloped and doctors in primary care centres tend to issue excessive prescriptions. Some progress has been achieved in improving incentives. This includes a further devolution of health care responsibilities and of revenue raising powers to the regions, and a relaxation of the constraint on the use of the State's transfers earmarked for health care. From 1998, a region which spends less than granted by the central government can retain the surplus, thus enhancing incentives to use resources better. Several regional pilot programmes, which focus on containing pharmaceutical costs and reducing public hospitals' waiting lists, have proved to be successful.[66]

Table 14. **Health care provision and expenditure**

Latest available year

	Total expenditure on health as a percentage of GDP	Total expenditure on pharmaceutical goods as a percentage of total expenditure on health	Doctors per 10 000 inhabitants	Pharmacists per 10 000 inhabitants	Average bed occupancy (%)	Nurses per available hospital bed
United States	13.9	10.0	27.1	7.0	66.0	1.7
Germany	10.7	12.3	34.5	5.7	76.2	0.6
France	9.6	17.2	29.8	10.0	81.9	0.4
Italy	7.6	19.4	57.7	9.6	73.4	0.8
United Kingdom	6.8	16.9	16.8	5.9	n.a.	1.7
Belgium	7.6	18.4	28.9	13.7	83.6	0.8
Greece	8.6	21.3	39.6	7.8	69.4	0.7
Ireland	6.3	10.6	21.3	7.2	83.2	1.3
Netherlands	8.5	10.9	25.9	1.7	87.7	n.a.
Portugal	7.9	26.9	30.6	7.4	73.5	1.1
Spain	**7.4**	**20.7**	**42.2**	**10.6**	**76.7**	**0.8**
Turkey	4.0	31.6	11.3	3.1	59.2	0.3
EU average	8.7	15.2	32.1	8.1	79.5	0.7
OECD average	10.0	9.8	27.7	6.9	76.1	0.9

Source: OECD Health Data.

Improving the sharing of experience between the regional and central health care institutions seems necessary to take full advantage of these pilot programmes. On the other hand, the 1998 personal income tax reform removed the proportional tax credit for health expenditure (15 per cent) but has made contributions to private health insurance tax exempt.[67] This provision should be re-examined since, in reducing the effective co-payment, it could raise demand for health care further.

Public hospitals

Considerable progress has been achieved in reducing the average waiting period to get treatment in public hospitals. This partly reflects the contracting out of some services to private providers and efforts to use the equipment more intensively. For instance, by adopting longer opening hours for surgery suites, the Basque Country has succeeded in bringing the average waiting period for a surgery from 84 days in 1993 to 59 in 1998. However, public hospitals' efficiency still suffers from poor management practices and incentives. Specifically, management is constrained by line budgeting which limits flexibility in the allocation of resources. Furthermore, incentives are skewed by the absence of a link between remuneration and performance, and by job tenure since doctors have a statute that is similar to that of a civil servant. Steps have been taken to improve incentives and reduce costs by introducing private management practices in several public hospitals. Three new hospitals will be managed by the private sector through 10-year contractual agreements. The 1999 budget law also envisages the transformation of some public hospitals into "public health foundations" which will benefit from greater management autonomy. Specifically, they will be able to hire personnel under more flexible contracts and allocate part of their budget to grant merit-based premiums. Nevertheless, few hospitals are expected to change status in the short term while rapid progress in this direction would be desirable.[68] Furthermore, quality of services could also be improved by giving the patient free choice of provider, and adopting simultaneously "the money follows the patient" principle. While public health care could still be provided without charge, competition between hospitals should promote cost-effective treatment.[69] Changes in the quality and costs of health services should be closely examined by the National Health Institute and by other regional governments. Reforming the incentives and financing of public health care centres along these lines would also help in this respect. Better preventive care would improve health outcomes and reduce pressures on specialised care departments.

Pharmaceuticals

Expenses on pharmaceuticals account for a significantly larger share of total health care spending than in most other OECD countries and have continued to grow steadily.[70] The exclusion of 800 products from the social security system's eligibility list in September 1998 has failed to restrain expenditure, which rose by 11.1 per cent in the first ten months of 1999. This partly reflects a substitution towards other, often more expensive, drugs. More promising, as international experience shows, would be the promotion of the use of generics accompanied by the introduction of a reference price system for pharmaceuticals. This will actually be adopted in the near future. To reap the maximum benefit of these measures, the period required to approve generics should be reduced and the reference price system should be extended to a wide range of pharmaceuticals. Also wholesalers' and pharmacists' margins (9.6 and 27.9 per cent respectively) could be reduced, either by cutting further these administratively set margins or by enhancing competition.[71] As a complement, excessive consumption should be lowered. In this regard, the National Health Institute has implemented a system to monitor doctors' prescription practices and patients' consumption. A similar system has been introduced in the Basque Country but suffers from the absence of sanctions for excessive prescriptions (expenses on pharmaceuticals have grown by 17 per cent in this region during the first five months of 1999). Abolishing the free access of pensioners to pharmaceuticals, possibly associated with the intro-duction of means-tested co-payments, would be another option to restrain drug over-consumption and fraud.[72] The introduction of daily dosage for pharmaceuti-cals could also be envisaged.

Public employment has remained stable

The process of decentralisation has not reduced the number of civil servants in Spain during the 1990s (Figure 19). For the public sector as a whole (excluding public enterprises[73]), more than 300 000 jobs have been created since 1990, though no further increases occurred since 1997. In order to restrain current outlays and achieve the Maastricht convergence criteria, the central government only replaces one out of every four permanent positions lost by normal job separations (retirement or quits). As a result, the number of central government and social security administration employees has dropped by more than 10 per cent since the 1997 peak. However, the increase in local and especially regional government employment roughly matched this decrease, revealing duplications in the devolution process to autonomous communities. Better incentives for labour mobility across regions should help avoid this problem. The recourse to temporary jobs in the central administration shows that the strict "one-to-four" rule cannot be effectively applied much longer without more flexibility and func-tional mobility, since bottlenecks are bound to appear in some government bodies. A new regulation on public sector employment has been presented to the Parliament (Estatuto de la Función Pública) that will homogenise salaries across cen-tral and local government bodies for similar workers, introduce new methods of personal management and introduce performance-related pay. The new system does not tackle other incentive problems due to life-long careers. Moreover, the

Figure 19. **Public employment**
Thousands persons

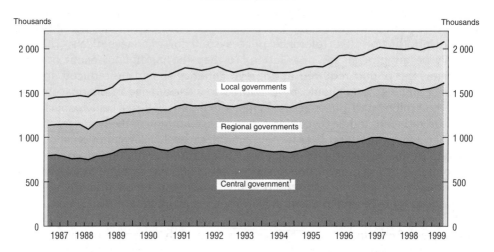

1. Including social security.
Source: Labour Force Survey (EPA).

traditional access system to public employment that relies on comprehensive examinations rather than on the assessment of an individual's ability to perform well on a specific post, remains in place.

Summary of recommendations for structural reform

In 1998-99, significant steps were made in critical areas of structural reform that will further liberalise the Spanish economy. Wide-ranging reforms have been implemented mainly to enhance product market competition and improve the functioning of capital markets, while the privatisation process has been further stepped up. The next round of reforms needs to consolidate the progress made so far in these areas and, most importantly, ensure a lasting improvement in the labour market and secure the sustainability of the pension system. To take advantage of policy complementarities, reforms would have to be comprehensive and systematic, covering a wide range of structural policies. They will, thus, be mutually reinforcing and will further enhance the macroeconomic prospects of the economy. Table 15 provides a summary of recent reforms, a follow-up on the recommendations of previous surveys, and a synthesis of options for further structural reform.

Table 15. Recommendations for further structural reform

Based on previous and current *Surveys* and action taken since early 1998

Previous *Survey*	Action taken	Current *Survey*
I. Labour market		
A. Reform employment protection provisions		
a) Severance payments remain among the highest in the OECD and should be reduced significantly.	New permanent contracts for targeted groups have been extended until 2000.	Undertake comprehensive reform of employment protection legislation, encompassing core workers.
b) Ensure that the decisions of the labour courts concerning severance payments conform to the spirit of the existing legislation.		Same as previous *Survey*.
c) Eliminate the administrative approval for collective dismissals.		Same as previous *Survey*.
d)		Streamline existing incentives to use permanent contracts through lower social security contributions, to minimise displacement effects.
B. Reform unemployment benefit system		
a) Incentives to job search need to be further enhanced.	Unemployment coverage has been extended for some long-term unemployed older than 45.	Monitor that this measure does not affect job search incentives.
b) Review the replacement rates.		Consider taking into account severance payments when compensating the unemployed for the loss of a job.
c) Maintain work incentives.		Restrict eligibility conditions of the unemployment subsidy programme for the rural sector to enhance regional labour mobility.
C. Increase labour cost and working-time flexibility		
a) Collective bargaining needs to take advantage of the potential new flexibility in negotiations and permit wages to reflect the economic circumstances.	Opting-out clauses have been included in provincial collective agreements, although they have hardly been used.	Attempt to reach an agreement to suppress sector and provincial levels of wage deals. This will enhance wage flexibility, firms' competitiveness and the regional mobility of labour.
b)	Unemployment insurance contribution rates were cut by 0.25 percentage point.	Lift social security contribution ceilings to reduce labour costs of the low paid.
c)		Improve the flexibility of the new part-time permanent work contract.
d)		Regional initiatives to reduce working time should be discouraged because they raise labour costs and impede employment gains.

Table 15. Recommendations for further structural reform (cont.)

Based on previous and current Surveys and action taken since early 1998

Previous Survey	Action taken	Current Survey
D. Enhance active labour market policies		
a) Unemployment benefits should be linked to training and/or work-fare.		Same as previous Survey.
b)		Enhance monitoring of the effectiveness of active labour market programmes.
E. Improve labour force skills and competencies		
a) Training programmes should maximise work experience.		Same as previous Survey.
II. Product markets		
A. Enhance product market competition		
a)	Notification of merger plans was made compulsory. Preparation of a new competition law that would increase the resources and powers of the competition authorities.	Implement rapidly the envisaged law. Consider merging the *Tribunal* and the *Servicio de Defensa de la Competencia* to set up a single independent competition authority.
b) Water.	Government's proposal to reform the Water Law and to introduce a market for water for some users.	Introduce more rational pricing for water and consider extending the market of property rights for all water resources.
c) Land: Relax restrictive land-use regulations which reduce worker mobility.		Simplify the criteria and reduce the waiting period for obtaining building permits.
d) Enhance competition of postal services.	New law that partly liberalises postal services.	
e) Transport: Consider auctioning long-term concessions of some sections of the train company.	Privatisation of the inter-city bus company *Enatcar*.	Open rail transport to competition and consider franchising in railways and urban transport.
f) Promote competition in sectors previously dominated by public enterprises.	Electricity: Privatisation of *Endesa*; cuts in regulated prices; wider choice for medium-sized consumers. Telecommunications: Several new operators allowed in basic and mobile telephony. The 1998 Hydrocarbon Law and its ammendments liberalise gas supply for large consumers. Elaboration of measures to enhance competition of oil retail distribution.	Enhance competition in generation. Improve transparency in the setting of interconnection charges. Streamline procedures and conditions to obtain a licence. Promote competition in the gas sector. Review the effects of cross-ownerships on the electricity and gas markets to avoid anti-competitive conduct.
g) Retail trade	Creation of a provincial advisory service to facilitate business start-ups.	Relieve regions' restrictions on shop-opening hours. Reduce further administrative steps to create a new business.

Table 15. **Recommendations for further structural reform** (cont.)
Based on previous and current *Surveys* and action taken since early 1998

Previous Survey	Action taken	Current *Survey*
B. Public subsidies		
a)		Lower public support to industry and concentrate on horizontal targets to prevent distortions to competition.
b)		Focus national support to agriculture more on restructuring incentives, and promote transparency of the criteria in the distribution of subsidies from State and regions.
III. Financial markets		
a)		Stay vigilant on prudential banking supervision, especially on risks related to Latin America, and on risk management practices of large credit institutions.
b)		Ensure a level-playing field in banking and promote ownership forms for savings banks that allow market-driven restructuring of the banking system.
c)	Reform of the Securities Markets Law that simplifies stock issuance, promotes asset securitisation and deregulates collective investment institutions.	
d)	New Venture Capital Law that increases tax incentives to venture capital funds and puts them under the supervision of the stock market regulator.	
IV. Public sector		
a) Pensions: Reduce the ratio of pension benefits relative to contributions in order to control future unfunded liabilities.	Increase in minimum pensions.	Review the generosity of pensions, further widen the pension base and reduce incentives to leave the labour market early. Consider complementing the pay-as-you-go system with a funded pension system. Speed up implementation and adopt global budgets instead of line budgeting for the remaining ones. Extend and speed up the authorisation of generics, while introducing a co-payment on pharmaceuticals for pensioners. Improve incentives for geographic mobility of civil servants to match increasing devolution of spending powers to regions by corresponding shifts in public employment.
b) Health care: Extend hospital management reforms.	Several hospitals transformed into "public health foundations"; others under study.	
c) Pharmaceuticals: Control expenditure.	Promotion of generics and foreseen implementation of a reference price system. Cut in distribution margins on pharmaceuticals.	
d) Public employment.	Draft law on public employment that introduces productivity incentives to civil servants.	

Source: OECD Secretariat.

III. Options for reforming the Spanish tax system

Until the mid-1970s government spending in Spain was fairly low by international comparison, keeping tax pressure considerably below the OECD average. However, after the 1975 shift to democracy and up until the late 1980s, taxation rose sharply to finance escalating government expenditure. Tax reforms, implemented until the beginning of the 1990s aimed mainly at endowing Spain with a modern tax system, and to raise funds to meet increasing demand for public services. Major steps in this process were the 1978 personal and corporate income tax reforms, the introduction of VAT after the accession to the European Union in 1986, and the 1991 reform of the personal income tax. At the same time, the tax system was subject to a number of pressures: coping with a political commitment to decentralise spending functions and taxation; pursuing distributional objectives; and providing aid to activities and constituencies in distress. Second-generation tax reforms, comprising the 1995 corporate and the 1998 personal income tax reforms, aimed at tax simplification, promoting tax neutrality and enhancing incentives for work, saving, risk-taking and investment.

Recent changes in the tax system have achieved progress in streamlining taxation, reducing compliance costs and redressing previous distortions resulting from tax progressivity and lack of neutrality. Despite improvements, the tax system still contains imbalances, reflected in a relative strong tax pressure on labour income, lack of neutrality in the taxation of savings, preferential corporate tax regimes of questionable efficiency, and weaknesses in tax decentralisation. The first section of the chapter reviews the economic and social context in which tax policy has been designed and will need to evolve in the future. The second section discusses the interactions of the tax system with main markets and institutions and then provides an assessment of its effectiveness in promoting growth, equity and cost-efficient tax collection. The third section weighs the resulting trade-offs in tax policy design and draws out the main options for further tax reform.

Forces shaping tax policy

Spending pressures were subdued in the 1990s, but will rise again

Between 1975 and the early 1990s total government expenditure – driven by spending on welfare programmes and on public investment – rose by more than one percentage point of GDP annually (Table 16), reaching 45 per cent of GDP in 1992. The rise in government outlays was initially matched by a significant increase in social security contributions and in personal income tax revenue. Subsequently, increasing public spending was covered by a rise in consumption taxes, with a considerable tax hike due to the introduction of VAT. Owing to the rapid rise in spending, Spain had, in 1990, a tax ratio only somewhat below the European average, starting from a level almost twice as low in 1975, and considerably higher than in non-European OECD countries (Figure 20). Over the 1990s, policy aimed at fiscal consolidation to fulfil the Maastricht treaty criteria. This was achieved largely by reining in government expenditure – especially on investment – rather than by raising the tax burden. Hence, in contrast to many other OECD countries, Spain's tax ratio stabilised.

However, the tax system could come under strain again in the future. As in most other OECD countries, population ageing could threaten the sustainability of the social security system. Thanks to a still young age structure of the population – owing to the comparatively later arrival of the "baby boom" generation in Spain – sustainability of the social security system is ensured in the short run. Starting from around 2005, however, the liabilities of the system are

Table 16. **Changes in general government expenditure and revenues[1]**

As a per cent of GDP

	1975 level	1975-80	1980-85	1985-92	1992-98
Total expenditure	**22.8**	**6.8**	**6.3**	**7.2**	**-2.8**
Consumption	11.3	2.9	1.5	2.6	-1.0
Transfers	8.0	3.9	1.3	1.8	-0.9
Subsidies	0.7	0.4	0.3	-0.2	0.2
Interest	0.3	0.2	1.8	2.0	0.1
Investment	2.6	-0.5	1.4	1.0	-1.2
Total revenues	**22.8**	**5.3**	**4.0**	**5.8**	**-0.6**
Personal income tax	1.9	2.6	1.2	2.8	-0.9
Social security	9.9	2.9	-0.3	1.3	-0.5
Corporate income taxes	2.0	-0.4	0.2	0.6	0.4
Consumption taxes	6.9	-0.1	2.9	0.3	1.1
Other revenues	2.1	0.4	0.0	0.8	-0.7

1.   Changes are calculated from 3-year moving averages centered at the end points of each sub-period.
Source: OECD Secretariat.

Figure 20. **The tax burden**

As a per cent of GDP[1]

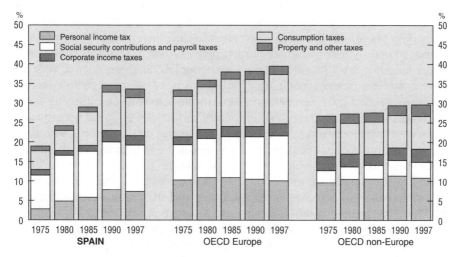

1. Three year centered moving average.
Source: OECD, *Revenue Statistics*.

projected to increase steadily, up to the middle of the century.[74] The pressures will become much stronger from 2025 onwards, when the "baby boom" generation retires. Holding the current contribution rates constant, the system is projected to generate a rising deficit, reaching 6 per cent of GDP in 2030 and a peak of nearly 9 per cent of GDP around 2050. Adjusting the parameters of the pension system as early as possible would help to smooth the fiscal cost of population ageing. As a complement to pension reform, the existing form of tax sheltering of saving for retirement could be preserved while tax incentives for other forms of saving instruments should be reconsidered. Some pressure on the tax system could also stem from the need to step up public investment to further upgrade infrastructure closer to the European Union standards – though increased private-sector participation could ease the budgetary impact.[75]

Tax reforms have aimed at boosting growth

Tax reforms during the 1990s have aimed at raising potential output by improving labour market performance and raising capital formation. The Spanish tax mix has a different balance compared with other European Union countries, with a relatively strong reliance on labour taxes, largely to finance social security expenditures,[76] and a relatively low share of consumption-based taxes. The comparatively large total share of personal income and labour taxes, as well as the bias towards employers' social security contributions, will need to be addressed in designing tax policy, given that unemployment is still pervasive. Several tax measures have been already implemented in the 1990s. The 1991 income tax reform included provisions to raise incentives for women to join the labour force by assessing taxes individually rather than at the family unit. To improve labour market performance by reducing labour costs, a small shift in the tax mix away from labour income was carried out in 1995. Social security contributions were reduced by 1 percentage point, in tandem with an offsetting increase in VAT rates. In addition, targeted temporary reductions in social security contributions were implemented as part of the 1997 labour market reform, with the aim of improving employment prospects of workers at the margin of the labour market (see Chapter II). Finally, with a view to rebalance the tax mix from direct to indirect taxes and to better reflect the costs and benefits of government-provided services, substantial increases in excise taxes and user fees were introduced in 1997. These measures, combined with the recent boom in private consumption have led to an increase in the share of indirect taxes in general government tax revenues from 30 per cent in 1994, to almost 34 per cent in 1999.

Reforms have also aimed to ease constraints on corporate financing and investment, to promote risk-taking, and to enhance firms' competitiveness (Box 5). The 1995 corporate income tax reform improved the neutrality of the tax system towards different financing instruments and investments. It also reduced the discrimination against foreign direct investment by Spanish firms by limiting the double taxation of dividends for inter-company share-holdings. Partly as a result, FDI outflows have risen by more than six-fold between 1995 and 1998. In addition, in June 1996, a set of tax measures was adopted to facilitate firms' access to capital markets. These measures included a change in the taxation of capital gains through the personal income tax, so as to limit financial "lock-in"[77] and enhance financial market deepening. A possibility was also given to companies to revalue their productive assets in line with inflation to bring depreciation expenses for tax purposes more into line with the true cost of capital, and thereby to boost investment. In 1997, the corporate income tax rate was cut from 35 to 30 per cent for small enterprises.

The devolution of revenue raising powers has lagged the rapid decentralisation of spending competencies

Until 1997, the decentralisation process was rapid but was characterised by an imbalance between tax assignments and expenditure functions. Since the establishment of regional governments by the 1978 constitution, regional governments' share in general government expenditure has risen steeply, from 3 per cent in 1981 to 25.7 per cent in 1997.[78] As a result, while Spain was a highly

Box 5.   **Main features of the 1995 corporate income tax reform and other measures affecting entrepreneurial activities**

- *Tax neutrality towards different sources of income was increased and compliance costs were reduced.* The 1995 reform abandoned the distinction between three types of incomes over which different tax rules were applying (operating income, net capital gains and net increases in assets). The 1995 law has identified the balance of the profit and loss account as the unique tax base. This measure also has the advantage of making the tax base easier to observe and verify.[1]
- *Distortions on investment decisions were reduced.* The 1995 CIT reform has allowed firms to value inventories adopting the LIFO (last in, first out) method, used in many other OECD countries. This method allows inventories to be valued at their historical costs, thus avoiding the taxation of changes in values reflecting inflation developments. Another step in this direction was taken in June 1996 when a voluntary revaluation of fixed assets (to account for inflation) was proposed to companies. This measure has allowed them to set more realistic depreciation expenditures, thus lowering their tax liabilities, and has facilitated their financing.[2] The 1995 law also allowed intangible assets (goodwill, trademarks) to be depreciated.
- *The neutrality of the tax system* vis-à-vis *financing instruments was increased.* The 1995 reform lessened the double taxation of dividends for inter-company shareholdings. The participation threshold to benefit from a tax exemption on dividends accruing from a participation in another company was brought down from 25 per cent to 5 per cent, if the participation was held for at least two years. In June 1996, the required holding period to benefit from an exemption of double taxation was reduced from 2 years to 1 year.
- *Tax constraints on the internationalisation of Spanish firms were eased.* The correction for international double taxation of dividends and capital gains was applied to corporations owning 5 per cent of the capital of foreign companies – instead of the 25 per cent limit contained in the 1978 law – during at least two years. The required holding period was reduced to one year in June 1996. Also, there were some legal changes to avoid the double taxation of revenues.
- *Measures to promote small and medium-sized enterprises were implemented.* The 1995 CIT law gave more freedom to SMEs in spreading capital depreciation expenses over time and also introduced tax incentives for investment. The 1997 budget law introduced another measure in favour of SMEs, lowering the tax rate which applies to them from 35 to 30 per cent – up to the first ESP 15 million of taxable income.[3]
- *Risk-taking and enterprise creation was encouraged.* The period during which firms can carry forward losses and offset them against future profits was raised from 5 to 7 years. The maximum period was raised to 10 years in the 1999 budget law.

---

1. See Serrano Leal (1996).
2. The previous revaluations took place in 1983. The 1997 voluntary revaluation was accompanied by a 3 per cent tax on the revaluation of companies' assets.
3. Firms with a turnover below ESP 250 million per year.

centralised country in the early 1980s, it stood close to the OECD average in 1997 when judged on the basis of regional and local governments' share in total expenditure (Figure 21). However, the devolution in revenue raising powers did not follow suit. Until 1997, fiscal devolution to the regions was confined to the so-called "ceded taxes", mainly on property. Tax revenues retained by the regions accounted for only 7 per cent of the central government total tax revenues (excluding social security contributions) in 1995. Fiscal discretion of regional governments was further limited by the fact that they could determine tax base or rates on only 22 per cent of their tax revenues, compared with around 90 per cent for Belgium, Denmark, Japan and Switzerland (OECD, 1999h). Some incentives for improving tax collection by the regions existed insofar as they could retain any positive deviation from the budgeted increase in receipts.[79] Overall, however, the bulk of regional financial resources continued to be provided by central government transfers, half of which were conditional – *i.e.* directed to specific purposes, such as the financing of social services or infrastructure investment.

Figure 21.   **Tax receipts and expenditure by regional and local governments**
1997[1]

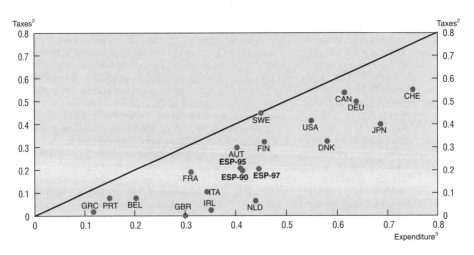

1. For Austria, Finland, Ireland, Netherlands, Sweden, Switzerland and United Kingdom: 1996. For Denmark, Greece, Italy and Portugal: 1995.
2. Direct and indirect taxes received by regional and local governments as a share of taxes received by the general government (excluding social security).
3. Total expenditure by regional and local governments as a share of general government expenditure (excluding social security and capital transfers).
Source: OECD, *National Accounts* and Bank of Spain, *Financial Accounts.*

The commitment to transfer further expenditure powers to the regions and to comply with the Spanish Stability Programme has given an impetus to enhance fiscal co-responsibility. The 1997-2001 financing system for the regions, which substituted lump-sum State transfers by locally-raised tax revenues, has been an important step towards improving incentives for sound management of public finance at the sub-national level. Incentives to trim expenditure result from the political costs of raising taxes now borne by regional governments. Specifically, since 1997, regional governments are able to modify the base and rates of the ceded taxes, though with some limitations. Moreover, limited powers to set marginal personal income tax rates and tax credits have been granted. However, the fear that tax competition could unduly undermine tax revenues of the regions has motivated the introduction of limits on the regions' taxing powers. Granting regional governments extensive powers to modify the base, rates and reliefs for more taxes would also make the tax system more complex and could widen tax loopholes. In addition, the principles of financial solidarity across regions and of resource sufficiency for the provision of public services – embodied in the Constitution – act as a limit to a rapid and more ambitious devolution of tax competencies. Overall, revenue-raising powers of the regions remain limited while further transfers in spending powers are planned. These concern the devolution of two main spending items, health and non-university education, which should be completed by 2004 for those regions where devolution has not yet happened.[80] In addition, regionalist parties are pushing for more devolution, both on the spending side – e.g. on social transfers or the management of airports – and for revenue raising and tax collection powers.

Main issues for strengthening the tax system

The complexity of tax laws: tax administration and compliance

Although much of the equipment and personnel endowment appears to be in place for an adequate functioning of the tax administration, in some respects effective enforcement of the tax laws could be strengthened. Reflecting an extensive use of computer technology and third party reporting requirements, collection costs are rather low by international standards – 1 per cent of tax revenues at the State level.[81] Compliance is also facilitated by an extensive reliance on withholding payments on wages and financial income. However, existing information on individuals' wealth (e.g. data from investment funds and bank accounts) is hardly used to verify income data, and the general feeling is that tax evasion – though difficult to estimate – is important.[82] As a matter of fact, tax fraud discovered over the two-year period 1996-98 amounted to ESP 2.2 billion (i.e. 7.6 per cent of the State's tax revenues).[83] Nevertheless, resources dedicated to the detection of undeclared activities are reported to be low compared to those devoted to the cross-checking of information on declared income flows. Furthermore, while the legal provisions call for severe penalties for tax evasion, these are applied only after a long delay, partly reflecting the lack of swift action by the judicial system.[84]

Enforcement problems also partly reflect the complexity of the tax law, which embodies many exemptions, deductions and special regimes.[85] It multiplies the opportunities for overstating expenditures and misrepresenting the characteristics of the tax unit, thus exacerbating tax evasion.[86] It also raises compliance costs and generates uncertainty. A survey revealed that in 1998 only 16 per cent of taxpayers filed their personal income tax return themselves and, because of the difficulties to adjust withholding payments to final tax liabilities in the presence of a plethora of deductions and exemptions, 73 per cent of taxpayers were entitled to tax refunds in 1998.[87] In addition, frequent changes in the tax law, in particular on capital income, may have undermined the predictability of the tax system.

The 1998 personal income tax reform was a significant step towards the simplification of the tax system. It streamlined deductions, reduced the number of tax brackets, and raised the income threshold below which an individual is no longer required to file a tax return (Box 6). The government expects that this will reduce compliance and administrative costs as well as tax evasion. Resources freed within the tax administration will be largely reallocated towards further enhancing assistance to taxpayers. Continued improvements of the Agencia's communication technology will also help to reduce compliance costs and achieve further progress in reducing the processing delays of tax returns.[88] Furthermore, the creation of the Consejo de Defensa del Contribuyente in 1996 and of the Estatuto del Contribuyente in March 1998 should help to reduce taxpayers' uncertainty by introducing maximum time limits on tax inspections, prescriptions and refunds.[89] Efforts to fight against tax evasion have also been intensified, in particular by regrouping the existing resources within the tax administration into a single unit (ONIF) and by better co-ordinating tax collection and tax inspection activities, in line with the Plan de Control Tributario Coordinado. Stricter limits to the change in tax residence (within and outside the country) and on financial transactions with non residents, aimed at reducing tax liabilities (in particular to avoid "coupon washing"), have also been introduced.[90] Enhanced tax responsibility of territorial governments could also help, by bringing the tax administration closer to taxpayers.

The corporate income tax, social security contributions and the value-added tax still embody multiple rates and tax reliefs which broaden the scope for tax avoidance. Progressivity in the corporate income tax (30 per cent for small firms, 35 for large ones) could lead to under-invoicing in order to be eligible for the lower rates and the self-employed are still taxed under the personal income tax, according to objective criteria rather than the realised income. In addition,

---

Box 6. **Main objectives of the 1991 and 1998 personal income tax reforms**

The 1991 personal income tax reform

- *The tax treatment of families became more neutral.* Married couples were given the option of filing separate returns, while the previous system aggregated incomes and filing was jointly. The new system reduces disincentives to labour force participation of household partners.
- *The tax base was broadened.* New sources of income were brought into the tax base (*e.g.* in-kind benefits).
- *Long-term savings were given tax incentives.* The taxation of undistributed profits of private investment funds was brought more into line with that existing in other EU countries. In particular, the legislation exempted investors from all withholding taxes on undistributed profits earned in the fund and only applied the capital gains tax when the resources were withdrawn from the fund. Long-term capital gains concerning investment held for more than 10 years were in general exempted.

The 1998 personal income tax reform

- *The tax burden has been reduced, and incentives to work enhanced.* Marginal rates were lowered, from 56 to 48 per cent for the top income bracket and from 20 to 18 for the lowest. The number of tax brackets was also reduced, from 10 to 6. Taxpayers with income up to ESP 3 million (accounting for 80 per cent of total taxpayers) should see their tax liabilities reduced by 15 to 30 per cent.
- *Neutrality across various types of incomes has been improved.* Labour and capital income have been put on a more equal footing, as most partial exemptions and credits on financial saving income were curtailed. Capital income, except long-term capital gains, has been integrated into the tax base, with possibilities of cross-compensation between losses and gains. Most partial exemptions on capital gains and income have been removed.
- *Neutrality across different saving instruments has been improved.* The reform also made significant progress in harmonising tax rates and withholding rates on income from different financial assets held during the same period.* The reform maintained, however, preferential treatment of long-term financial saving instruments and owner-occupied housing.
- *An exempted living standard minimum has replaced a vast set of tax reliefs.* The personal income tax previously included an extensive set of tax reliefs, which reduced its productivity, created horizontal inequities, and provided broad scope for tax avoidance. The 1998 reform introduced a tax-exempt living standard minimum – *minimo exento* –which takes into account the characteristics of the tax unit. It substituted for most existing tax breaks (*e.g.* health and education expenditure, renting charges, care for the handicapped, child-care expenses).
- *Compliance and collection costs have been lowered, thus freeing resources to fight tax evasion.* Withholding payments were redesigned to take into account individuals' characteristics, and thus fit better with effective tax liabilities. The threshold below which individuals are not required to fill a tax return was raised

(continued on next page)

(continued)

from ESP 1.2 million in 1998 to 3.5 million. These two measures are expected to allow for a 5 million decrease in the number of tax returns to be filed (*i.e.* by about one third of total personal income tax returns), and tax refunds. The assessment of taxable income was also made more easily verifiable by the suppression of the imputed income of owner-occupied housing. Freed resources will be reallocated to activities of advising and assisting taxpayers, and to more effectively fight against tax fraud.

---

* A 20 per cent rate is applied on capital gains on assets held for at least two years.

both for the personal and the corporate taxes, rules applied in the Basque Country and the Navarra region differ from the rest of Spain, thus increasing the complexity of the tax system. While the value added tax rules are the same for the whole Spanish territory, a large number of goods are taxed at reduced or super-reduced rates. For small enterprises with poor book-keeping, VAT on differentially taxed products cannot be accounted for separately. The tax liability must thus be determined by applying presumptive methods, an approach that increases the difficulty of monitoring compliance. The social security system is also characterised by a proliferation of partial exemptions or reduced rates and different ceilings on contributions according to the situation of the worker (age, qualification, etc.).

Taxation and labour market performance

Taxes on labour income account at present for close to 60 per cent of general government revenues. In 1997, the overall tax wedge (personal income tax and social security contributions) of a single average production worker (APW) was 39 per cent of gross labour costs. Employers' and employees' social security contributions accounted together for two-thirds of the tax wedge (Figure 22, panel A), with the major part (60 per cent) corresponding to employers' contributions. The tax wedge is close to the OECD average, and thus well below the European average. During the 1990s the tax wedge increased by two percentage points, nearly as much as on average in the European Union (Figure 22, panel B). Concerning marginal tax rates, Spain is again significantly below the EU average, with a marginal tax wedge for an average production worker of 44 per cent in 1997 (Figure 22, panel C).

Cross-country empirical studies have confirmed that rising tax wedges on labour income may partly account for the increase in structural unemployment observed in many OECD countries. A higher tax wedge raises labour costs and can

Figure 22. **Tax wedge on labour**[1]
As a percentage of gross labour costs[2]

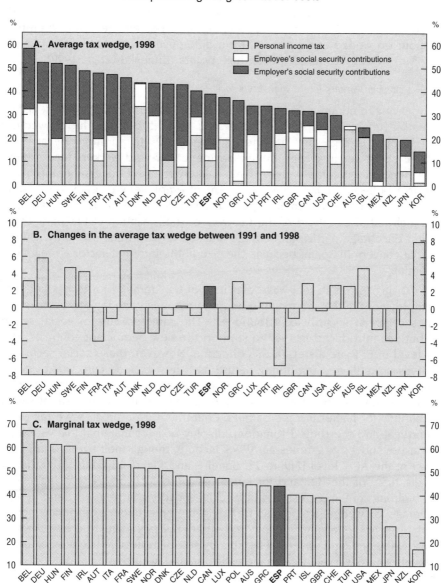

1. For a single individual at the income level of the average production worker.
2. Gross wage plus employers' contributions.
Source: OECD, *The Tax/Benefit Position of Employees.*

lead to a reduced demand for labour. Unless labour supply is fully wage-inelastic and wages are fully flexible, the increasing tax burden will be in part shifted into higher pre-tax wages and lead to a lower level of employment. A panel data estimate for 19 OECD countries suggests that a 10 percentage point difference in the labour tax wedge could account for a difference in structural unemployment rates of up to as much as 1.5 percentage points (Elmeskov *et al.*, 1999).

Low-paid workers face a high tax wedge

Owing to minimum payments and to contribution ceilings, which apply to both employees' and employers' social security contributions, the tax wedge on labour income is regressive (Figure 23, panel A).[91] In addition, because of a minimum social security contribution payment, low-paid workers face a higher-than-average marginal tax wedge.[92] This is likely to affect adversely employment of the low skilled. Though only 3 per cent of employees receive the minimum wage, many more workers could be excluded from the formal labour market due to the high initial threshold of the tax wedge. High taxation of low-paid workers may thus encourage participation in the untaxed underground economy. This is of particular concern in Spain, because the size of the informal sector appears to be substantial.

Owing to a high real-wage elasticity of the demand for low-skilled workers, employment of this group could be quite responsive to targeted cuts in taxes or rates of social security contributions.[93] The targeted cuts in social security contributions introduced in 1997 to support the new permanent contracts with a lower level of EPL are a step in this direction. However, these social security tax incentives are still of a temporary nature and they exclude core worker groups. Enhancing across-the-board progressivity of the tax wedge on labour income in a revenue-neutral way might call for a quite substantial increase in social security contributions for higher income earners. Countries with a progressive tax wedge, like Portugal and the United Kingdom, display a *higher* marginal tax wedge than Spain at beyond 1.5 to 2 times an APW's income, though their average tax wedge is lower at the APW level (Figure 23, panel B and Figure 22 panel A). If the real-wage elasticity of the demand for labour declines for workers with higher-level skills, building some progressivity into social security contributions (and hence in the average tax wedge) would also be advisable on economic efficiency grounds. Cutting taxes at the low-income/low-skill end of the pay scale, where workers face an elastic demand, and offsetting tax cuts by steeper effective tax rates at income/ skill levels where workers face an inelastic demand, would bring about a decrease in the overall excess burden of labour taxation.[94]

Tax wedges interact with labour market rigidities

While Spain has a relatively low tax wedge by European standards, its adverse impact on employment may have been exacerbated by a number of

Figure 23. **The total marginal tax wedge**
1998, per cent

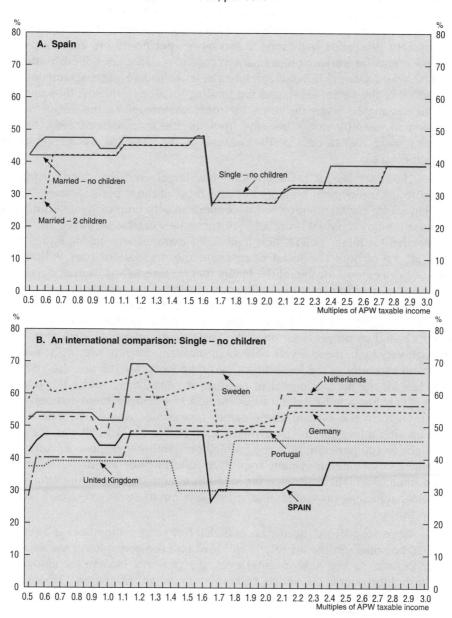

Source: OECD, *The Tax/Benefit Position of Employees.*

rigidities that reduced firms' incentives to resist upward pressure on wages and thereby facilitated forward shifting of taxation into labour costs. These rigidities include: i) a low level of product-market competition in sheltered sectors – that was prevalent until at least Spain's accession to the European Union; ii) restrictive employment protection legislation – and more specifically the generous severance payments for workers on permanent contracts – that considerably strengthened "insiders' power" in wage agreements; iii) collective wage agreements that are settled at the sector level, and are binding for all enterprises, thus putting a floor to negotiated wage increases for most companies in the sector; iv) the exclusion of unemployment benefits from taxable income until 1994, thereby stiffening wage resistance[95] partly because of the resulting weakening of job search incentives.

The 1994 labour market reform has largely redressed tax distortions related to unemployment benefits because most of them became taxed.[96] However, severance payments received in connection with employment security provisions still enjoy a partial tax relief.[97] Disincentives can be portrayed by "marginal effective tax rates" (METRs) on household extra income, taking into account the influence of both the social benefit and the tax system. They indicate the share of extra earned income of the family that is "taxed away", either because of withdrawal of unemployment benefits, cancellation of means-tested social benefits, or higher income taxes (Table 17). In the standard case of a single-earner (full-time or part-time) household, where the non-working member is not entitled to benefits based on previous earnings, the METRs are somewhat below 80 per cent. Although very high, these levels have been brought down to the OECD average, and stand currently at the low end for part-time work. METRs are also comparatively low for the second earner of two-earner households, where the principal earner either has a full-time job or is entitled to unemployment compensation. Nevertheless, in the case of single-earner households where part-time work is taken up after a long-run unemployment spell (Table 17, last column), the METR is still above 100 per cent, indicating a high probability that these workers could be caught in an unemployment trap. This reflects both withdrawal of means-tested unemployment assistance for long-run unemployed, and the structure of the personal income tax system that allows long-run unemployment assistance to remain tax-free.

Across-the-board income tax cuts that have come into effect as a result of the 1998 personal income tax reform will lead to a somewhat lower tax wedge on labour income. At the APW income level, the personal income tax amounts to one-third of the overall tax wedge, corresponding to approximately 13 per cent of gross labour costs. According to preliminary estimates, personal income tax relief under the 1998 reform would allow a 1.5 percentage point drop in the income tax component of the tax wedge, bringing the overall tax burden to 37.5 per cent of gross labour costs.[98] However, the interaction with labour-market rigidities might

Table 17. **Marginal effective tax rates[1] on additional income for one- and two-earner households**
1997

	Full-time employed[2]/ non-employed	Part-time employed[3]/ non-employed	Full-time employed[4]	Full-time employed/ part-time employed	Unemployed/ full-time employed	Unemployed[5]/ part-time employed without benefit entitlements	Part-time employed after 5 years of unemployment/non-employed
Spain	**78**	**77**	**23**	**19**	**23**	**19**	**159**
Netherlands	89	90	39	37	45	52	134
Finland	88	117	36	23	48	23	152
Sweden	88	79	37	42	43	42	154
Luxembourg	87	198	30	14	26	12	198
Switzerland	85	96	30	27	20	15	184
Czech Republic	85	162	19	2	22	15	162
Denmark	84	84	50	48	55	61	118
Germany	80	115	51	50	31	19	115
Portugal	79	174	21	13	14	11	174
Australia	78	60	29	15	78	60	60
Norway	77	77	47	43	42	35	142
France	76	69	28	38	29	30	133
Austria	76	135	30	21	32	43	135
Canada	75	105	37	33	34	29	131
Hungary	73	106	29	12	34	23	106
United Kingdom	72	93	28	20	60	55	93
Belgium	68	109	57	61	43	25	109
Ireland	68	83	32	25	20	38	60
United States	68	102	19	11	20	0	102
Italy	63	84	33	25	37	19	84
Iceland	63	139	44	56	27	49	139
Japan	60	133	12	10	10	7	133
Korea	55	129	13	9	2	1	129
Greece	54	104	30	30	66	118	104
Poland	48	58	19	17	19	17	91

1. Marginal effective tax rate = 1 – (net income in work – net income out of work)/change in gross income.
2. Earnings from full-time employment correspond to APW earnings.
3. Part-time employment corresponds to 16 hours or two days each week, and total earnings are 40 per cent of the APW level of earnings.
4. Applies to both earners.
5. Receiving a full-time unemployment benefit.
Source: OECD, Benefit systems and Work Incentives.

restrict the responsiveness of labour demand and supply to incentives created by reduced tax rates. To enhance the employment impact of tax cuts, an increase in after-tax income from work should not be reflected in increased after-tax replacement income for those out of work and receiving severance payments.[99]

Real estate taxes and tax preferences to owner-occupied housing limit labour mobility

Owing to restrictive urban land development regulations, which significantly restrict housing supply, home prices in Spain are among the highest in the OECD. Excessive reliance of local authorities on real estate taxes may reduce housing investment further, and raises home prices and market rents. With an average ratio of home value to median family income of 5.3, Spain is next only to Japan and the Netherlands (with ratios of 6.6 and 5.5 respectively), which suffer housing price pressures mainly due to high population density – as well as to restrictive planning in Japan. In addition, as a result of generous tax preferences granted to owner-occupied housing, the rental market for housing comprises less than 15 per cent of the existing residential housing stock (Dolado, González-Páramo and Viñals, 1997). Poor development of the housing rental market, high home prices which vary significantly across regions, weak job search incentives, are factors that jointly hamper the geographic mobility of labour and impede labour market adjustment. The low geographic mobility of workers prevents regional labour markets from absorbing labour market imbalances and raises the overall rate of unemployment.

Non-neutralities still exist in the taxation of savings

While the relationship between after-tax returns and the level of saving cannot easily be determined because the income and substitution effects work in opposite directions, empirical evidence suggests that the composition of household saving is quite sensitive to tax policy (see OECD, 1994c). In Spain, the tax system has encouraged investment in home ownership, insurance and pension schemes, as well as mutual funds. This has reduced the supply of finance for newly created, innovative and fast-growing enterprises. Further hindering the reallocation of funds between enterprises is the taxation of dividends, which could give firms an incentive to retain their earnings, while providing shareholders with more lightly taxed capital gains. The tax differentiation in favour of long holding periods may also reduce the liquidity of the Spanish stock market and hinder an efficient allocation of resources.

Preferential tax treatment of housing

Tax incentives for housing investment were reduced by the 1998 personal income tax reform but remain generous, both compared with other savings instruments and by international standards (Dolado, Gonzales-Paramo and Viñals,

1997). In 1996, more than one fourth of personal income taxpayers were entitled to a housing-related tax credit, and tax expenditure on owner-occupied housing amounted to 4.6 per cent of personal income tax revenues.[100] In the 2000 State Budget, they are projected to rise further, to 9.1 per cent of personal income tax revenues. These tax incentives are reflected in a very high rate of owner-occupied houses by international standards (Figure 24). By far the most important tax incentive on housing is the 15 per cent tax credit on loan costs (both interest and principal repayments), up to a ESP 225 000 limit.[101] This contrasts with the absence of any tax deductibility of interest on consumer credits. In addition, capital gains on owner-occupied dwellings are corrected for inflation developments, whereas those on financial assets are not, and they are tax-exempt if reinvested in housing. Furthermore, money invested in housing saving accounts gives right to a tax rebate. In principle, tax deductibility of home ownership cost should only apply if housing is consistently treated as an investment good, with imputed services from home ownership being taxed. However, from 1999 the returns to an owner-occupied main residence (imputed rent) are no longer taxed; in any case taxation was already low before 1999.[102]

This set of tax incentives on housing investment poses several problems. First, they have questionable distributional consequences since they benefit

Figure 24. **Owner-occupied housing in selected OECD countries[1]**
As a per cent ot the residential housing stock

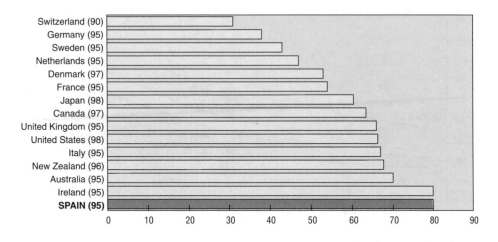

1. Data in brackets are the census year.
Source: National sources and OECD Secretariat.

disproportionately higher income groups. *Second*, given the low responsiveness of housing supply to demand – partly reflecting strict regulations on land use – existing tax provisions designed to encourage access to housing may largely be capitalised in higher house prices. *Third*, tax advantages on owner-occupied housing may contribute to the low geographic mobility of labour (Oswald, 1997). Finally, by favouring the allocation of saving towards real estate assets, the tax system may have a crowding-out effect on the availability of capital for other investment.

Distortions towards long-term saving concern mutual and pension funds, as well as life insurance

The preferential tax treatment of income from returns on some financial instruments up to the 1998 tax reform, combined with the decline in interest rates since the mid-1990s, has profoundly affected the composition of households' portfolios. The most striking feature has been the drop in time deposits in absolute terms since 1995 while mutual funds were booming (Figure 25). The personal income tax reform has reduced the tax bias in favour of mutual funds, both in terms of withholding taxes and tax rates, and has been reflected in a rebound in time deposits in early 1999. Specifically, withholding tax on deposit

Figure 25. **Composition of households' financial portfolio**
Billion euro

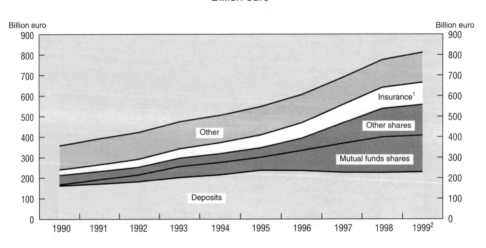

1. Including life insurance and pension funds.
2. Data for 1999 are second quarter data
Source: Bank of Spain, *Financial Accounts.*

income has been cut from 25 per cent to 18 per cent and the reform introduced a 20 per cent withholding tax on investment funds (they were not subject to with-holding payments before). In addition, the difference between the tax rate apply-ing to investment funds held for more than two years and deposits was cut significantly – from 35 to 13 percentage points for individuals taxed at the top rate (Table 18).

Progress towards greater tax neutrality has been a hallmark of the 1998 personal income tax reform. Broadening the "regular" taxable income base to include most financial income has been an important step towards the "com-prehensive income tax model" according to which tax neutrality is achieved when all sorts of income are taxed equally.[103] However, despite the reduction in tax distortions on financial assets, investment in pension funds and life insurance contracts continue to benefit from a preferential tax treatment. While there is a case for sheltering retirement savings, as a complement to pension reform, tax privileges granted to life-insurance contracts and mutual funds are less justifiable. Nevertheless, differences in tax rates on interest income and life insurance investment remain high, and pension fund contributions are deductible.[104] These differences continue to affect the composition of financial saving and, in turn, the financing of the economy since institutional investors differ from other financial intermediaries in their asset allocation choices. In particular, and partly for tax reasons, institutional investors tend to weight their portfolios heavily towards general government's and mature enterprises' securities.[105] Furthermore, con-trasting with the practice in many OECD countries, the Spanish tax system does not offer special incentives for direct share purchases . For individuals in the top income bracket, the combined corporate and personal tax burden on distributed profits far exceeds that on retained earnings (44 per cent *versus* a statutory 35 per cent for the corporate income tax and an even lower effective rate). Firms have thus an incentive to retain their earnings, while providing shareholders with lower taxed capital gains. Overall, the taxation on saving hinders the widening of share ownership and the reallocation of funds from mature, slow-growing, companies to more innovative firms.

The taxation of household saving continues to embody significant incen-tives for long holding periods after the 1998 IRPF reform. For the highest-income group, the tax rate applied on life insurance varies from 48 per cent for invest-ments held less than two years, down to 14.4 per cent for those held more than 8 years (Table 18). Other OECD countries also tax short-term capital gains more heavily than long-term ones. However, the threshold holding period to avoid this tax surcharge is generally shorter.[106] Incentives towards savings maintained over such a long period may create a "lock-in effect", because individuals have an incentive to hold assets for longer periods. This could limit the financing available for newly-created and dynamic firms, as well as reduce the liquidity of the Spanish capital markets.

Table 18. **Tax rates on financial saving**

By income bracket, 2000

	Tax bracket (in ESP thousand) and tax rate (in per cent)						Memorandum items: withholding rate
Income ceiling for the tax bracket	0-612	612-2 142	2 142-4 182	4 182-6 732	6 732-11 220	> 11 220	
Marginal personal income tax rate	18.0	24.0	28.3	37.2	45.0	48.0	
Financial products/income							
Held less than 2 years							
Bank accounts, life insurance contracts	18.0	24.0	28.3	37.2	45.0	48.0	18.0
Treasury bills	18.0	24.0	28.3	37.2	45.0	48.0	0.0
Private bonds	18.0	24.0	28.3	37.2	45.0	48.0	0.0
Capital gains on shares	18.0	24.0	28.3	37.2	45.0	48.0	0.0
Capital gains on mutual funds	18.0	24.0	28.3	37.2	45.0	48.0	20.0
Dividends[1]	16.0	22.0	26.0	34.0	41.0	44.0	18.0
Held more than 2 years							
Bank accounts	12.6	16.8	19.81	26.0	31.5	33.6	18.0
Housing savings schemes	12.6	16.8	19.81	26.0	31.5	33.6	18.0
Pension funds (lump-sum payment)[2]	10.8	14.4	17.0	22.3	27.0	28.8	18.0
Life insurance contracts (lump-sum payment)	10.8	14.4	17.0	22.3	27.0	28.8	18.0
Capital gains on shares	20.0	20.0	20.0	20.0	20.0	20.0	0.0
Capital gains on mutual funds	20.0	20.0	20.0	20.0	20.0	20.0	20.0
Held more than 5 years							
Life insurance contracts (lump-sum payment)	7.2	9.6	11.3	14.9	18.0	19.2	18.0
Held more than 8 years							
Life insurance contracts (lump-sum payment)	5.4	7.2	8.5	11.2	13.5	14.4	18.0

1. Taxes paid at the company level are included here, reflecting the partial imputation system which allows an individual to deduct a 40 per cent imputation credit against his tax liability. The system embodies a 26 per cent effective corporate rate, which contrasts with a 35 per cent statutory rate and a 30 per cent rate for SMEs.
2. Contributions to pension funds are deductible from the taxable income up to ESP 1.1 million or 20 per cent of labour income (the lowest amount). The ESP 1.1 million ceiling increases gradually for people older than 52, up to 2.2 million for a 65 years-old.

Source: OECD Secretariat.

Investment, entrepreneurship and the tax system

Low average effective corporate taxation but a rather high overall tax wedge on distributed profits and investment

Spain has a statutory corporate tax rate (35 per cent) very close to the EU average, though, as elsewhere in Europe, it displays a lower effective rate of corporate taxation as a result of a number of tax incentives. Estimates suggest that over 1990-96 the effective corporate tax rate has been 11 percentage points lower than the statutory rate (Figure 26), which is close to the average tax relief provided in the European Union.[107] Nevertheless, such international comparisons should be digested with great care.[108] Major corporate tax incentives are economy wide and take the form of investment tax credits. Targeted activities mainly include R&D expenses, staff training, and participation in foreign entities directly related to export activities. Moreover, a number of special sectoral and geographic corporate tax regimes exist.[109] The most important ones apply to banks and finance companies, mining companies, collective undertaking institutions, activities of cultural interest, small and medium sized enterprises (SMEs), foreign security holding companies, and companies subject to the Basque Country and

Figure 26. **Effective corporate taxation in the European Union**
Average 1990-96

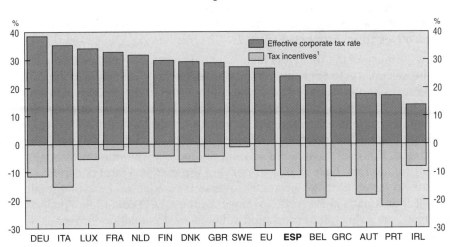

1. Difference between the effective corporate tax rate and the statutory corporate tax rate.
Source: Maastricht Accounting and Auditing Research and Education Center, April 1999.

Figure 27.   **Breakdown of gross corporate income tax liabilities**
1996

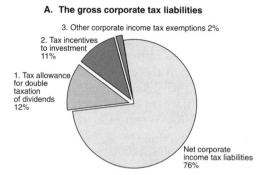

A. **The gross corporate tax liabilities**

3. Other corporate income tax exemptions 2%
2. Tax incentives to investment 11%
1. Tax allowance for double taxation of dividends 12%
Net corporate income tax liabilities 76%

B. **The structure of tax reliefs (2 + 3)**

A 7%
B 6%
C 1%
D 1%
E 3%
F 3%
G 34%
H 2%
I 29%
J 14%

Note: A: Canary Island special regime, B: Transitory 3-year tax relief for business start-ups in 1994 and 1997, C: Cooperative societies, D: Tax credit applying in Ceuta y Melilla, E: Tax relief for exporters of educational and cultural goods, F: Other corporate tax incentives, G: Carry over of tax exemptions, H: Tax relief for employment creation, I: Transitory 1996 5% tax credit on investment, J: General tax incentives to investment (R&D, training...).
Source: Ministry of Economy and Finance.

Navarra tax legislation, as well as to the Canary Islands special tax regime. In 1996, total tax expenditures amounted to 24 per cent of total gross corporate income tax liabilities (0.7 per cent of GDP) – with half of them accounted for by the various tax incentives to investment (Figure 27).[110]

Because of the relatively high marginal tax rates for higher-income taxpayers, the overall tax wedge on physical investment – reflecting both corporate income taxes and personal income taxes at the level of the individual investor – is rather high in international comparison (Table 19).[111] Spain applies a partial imputation system for distributed profits that provides tax credits for dividends of domestic origin. The taxation of dividends adds to the overall tax wedge on investment. However, taking into account the more favourable tax treatment (at a 20 per cent flat rate, instead of a 48 per cent top marginal rate) of capital gains on assets held for at least two years, the overall tax wedge on investment falls by a third. It then stands close to the average for the OECD countries. Finally, lack of systematic indexing of depreciation allowances to inflation increases the tax wedge by artificially inflating taxable profits. Specifically, in Spain the tax allowance for depreciation is based on assets' purchase values. From time to time, the government allows companies to revalue their assets. This occurred in 1983 and 1997.[112]

Table 19. **Marginal effective tax wedges on physical investment, R&D and human capital[1]**

1998, in per cent

	Sources of financing[2]			Physical assets[3]			Overall weighted average[4]	R&D,[5] 1996		Human capital, 1996	
	Retained earnings	New equity	Debt	Machinery	Building	Inventories		Short lived	Long lived	Training[6]	Tertiary studies
Spain, 1999a[7]	3.7	2.7	2.0	2.7	3.2	3.4	3.0	-7.7	-1.3	1.6	-0.1[9]
Spain, 1999b[8]	1.7	2.7	2.0	1.7	2.1	2.2	1.9	-8.0	-1.8	0.8	..
Canada	4.7	5.7	1.4	2.5	4.3	5.5	3.7	-4.0	-0.4	1.1	-0.7
France	4.4	8.5	0.8	2.6	4.1	4.8	3.5	-1.1	0.1	0.6	0.0
Japan	4.5	7.4	-0.3	1.8	5.1	3.7	3.1	-0.2	0.6	0.5	0.7
Luxembourg	4.0	2.7	1.8	2.4	3.0	4.7	3.1	1.7	1.7	1.6	..
Denmark	2.4	3.2	2.9	2.2	2.6	3.8	2.7	-1.7	0.6	1.6	0.0
Australia	2.6	2.5	2.5	2.1	2.7	3.4	2.6	-6.0	-1.0	0.9	-0.6
United States	2.0	5.7	1.7	1.7	3.0	2.6	2.3	-3.8	-0.2	1.0	0.0
Ireland	1.9	3.4	2.4	1.8	2.1	3.1	2.2	0.8	0.8	0.8	-0.8
United Kingdom	2.2	2.8	1.8	1.7	2.1	3.1	2.2	0.8	0.8	0.8	..
Netherlands	0.6	6.3	3.0	1.8	2.3	2.0	2.0	0.8	-0.1	1.0	-0.5
Sweden	2.4	3.4	1.0	1.7	2.1	2.5	2.0	-3.6	1.1	1.0	-1.8
New Zealand	1.8	1.8	1.8	1.7	1.5	2.3	1.8	1.1	0.7	0.0	-0.7
Finland	2.5	1.0	0.6	1.4	1.9	2.9	1.8	0.7	0.3	0.7	-0.1
Italy	2.2	2.5	0.0	1.0	1.8	3.1	1.7	0.7	0.3	0.0	-0.7
Portugal	2.1	4.4	-0.1	1.5	1.5	2.0	1.6	0.3	-0.2	-0.3	..
Iceland	2.2	2.7	2.2	1.0	1.6	2.3	1.5	-0.2	1.3	1.0	-0.3
Switzerland	0.5	4.1	1.3	1.3	1.6	1.7	1.4	1.3	0.5	0.4	..
Norway	1.3	1.3	1.3	1.0	1.7	2.0	1.3	0.5	0.1	0.0	-0.4
Germany	1.4	0.9	-0.1	1.1	1.7	1.3	1.3	0.0	0.0	-0.2	..
Greece	1.8	1.8	-0.7	0.9	0.5	2.4	1.1	-0.6	-0.6	-0.6	..
Belgium	1.6	3.0	0.2	0.1	0.8	3.1	1.0	-0.5	-0.5	-0.5	..
Mexico	1.5	1.5	0.2	0.9	0.9	1.3	1.0	-0.3	-0.3	..	..
Austria	1.0	3.2	0.2	0.0	1.1	2.6	0.9	-2.4	-0.8	-0.1	-0.8

1. These indicators show the degree to which the personal and corporate income tax systems scale up (or down) the real pre-tax rate of return that must be earned on an investment, given that the household can earn a 5 per cent real rate of return on a demand deposit. See OECD (1991b) for discussion of this methodology. Calculations are based on top marginal tax rates for the personal income tax and a 2 per cent inflation rate.
2. The weighted average uses the following weights: machinery 50 per cent, buildings 28 per cent, inventories 22 per cent.
3. The weighted average uses the following weights: retained earnings 55 per cent, new equity 10 per cent, debt 35 per cent.
4. The weighted average uses weights indicated in footnotes 2 and 3.
5. The weighted average uses the following weights: 5 per cent machinery, 5 per cent buildings and 90 per cent current expenditure across assets and weights in footnote 3 for financing.
6. The weighted average uses weights in footnote 3 for financing.
7. Using the 1999 top marginal personal income tax rate.
8. Using the 1999 top marginal personal income tax rate and a 20 per cent flat rate for capital gains.
9. Using the 1998 personal income tax parameters.
Source: Calculated by the OECD Secretariat.

A level playing field for physical investment but unbalanced incentives to invest in intangible assets

Compared with other OECD countries, the tax system in Spain shows a higher degree of neutrality across physical capital assets and sources of investment financing (Table 19).[113] Nevertheless, the relatively high taxation of distributed profits still provides a disincentive to finance investment by new equity issues. Even after the 1999 personal income tax cuts, the tax system drives a combined corporate and personal income tax wedge of 53 per cent on distributed profits (Figure 28), suggesting that there might be room for further enhancing tax neutrality towards corporate financing decisions.[114] This is most obvious in the case of the flat-rate taxation of long-term capital gains, which biases financing towards retained earnings by reducing the tax wedge considerably below that for new equity. This feature of the tax system is likely to distort investment decisions of "immature" and rapidly growing companies that may not be able to generate sufficient retained earnings to finance their investment plans.

As elsewhere in the OECD, investment in R&D receives preferential tax treatment, which is set to increase further.[115] They are more generous than those for training. The incentive to invest in firm-specific training is low, since the level

Figure 28. **Combined corporate and personal income tax wedge on distributed profits**

1998, resident top earner individuals

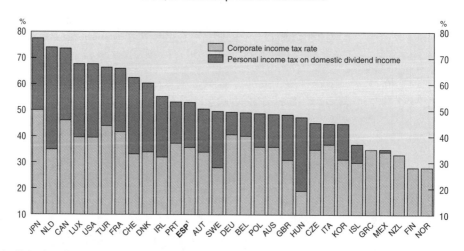

1. Using the 1999 marginal personal income tax rate for top earners.
Source: OECD Secretariat.

of the tax credit for employee training is set at only 5 per cent of the corresponding expenses. As workers that have been trained by firms may leave at any time,
the firm cannot be sure to recoup its training investments, which could lead to an
underinvestment in training. Though this is typically thought to hold true mainly
for general training, in practice the same applies also to firm-specific training by
competitive enterprises that use quite similar technologies.[116] Moreover, as
unemployment is still pervasive in Spain, this kind of intangible investment might
create a social pay off even more sizeable than elsewhere by enhancing bonding
of workers to firms – owing to better tuning of workers' abilities to firm requirements. It is noteworthy that the Basque Country already provides a more favourable tax treatment of training expenses (10 per cent tax credit) and is suffering
less acute unemployment problems than the rest of Spain. Household-sponsored
investment in tertiary education also receives a favourable tax treatment in Spain,
though rather less than elsewhere in the OECD. By taxing away less of the
increase in lifetime earnings induced by higher education, the tax rate flattening
of the 1998 personal income tax reform is expected to further enhance incentives
in this area.

Tax incentives granted to SMEs may hinder entrepreneurship

As in other OECD countries, special tax schemes targeted at SMEs
(Annex I) aim at correcting perceived cost disadvantages. These involve mainly
difficulties in raising finance, as well as coping with regulations and cumbersome
tax procedures. Regarding unincorporated business and the self-employed, it can
be argued that, though the new simplified rules go in the right direction and
should lead to a reduction in potential tax fraud, the "forfaitaire" tax system
(based on activity indicators) has outlived its initial purpose of simplifying tax
compliance for micro-enterprises. Moreover, the "forfaitaire" system is detrimental to horizontal taxpayer equity, as firms whose profits are underestimated by the
relevant activity indicators may free ride on the system. As the use of accounting
is becoming more widespread and "simplified direct estimation" schemes of tax
assessment are being introduced, the "forfaitaire" system should eventually be
phased out.

Regarding corporate businesses, the progressivity built into the tax system through the reduced rate of 30 per cent may distort incentives for tax compliance. Even though truncating business firms only for tax purposes might not be
worthwhile as it involves higher management costs, the existence of corporate tax
thresholds may induce tax avoidance through under invoicing and revenue under
reporting. Moreover, corporate tax progressivity could hamper business expansion. It treats profits and losses asymmetrically, by taxing increased profits more
heavily but not making appropriate allowance for losses. This feature of the
corporate tax may discourage risk taking and hence weaken entrepreneurship.

Existing corporate tax regimes could generate distortions in competition

Special corporate income tax regimes apply to the three historic Basque Country territories (Alava, Guipuzcoa, Vizcaya) and to Navarra. They provide several more generous tax incentives to companies than the general regime, as outlined in Box 8 below. In the case of the Basque Country special corporate tax regime, the general investment tax credit and the extra tax relief granted for business start-ups seem very generous and may lead to inefficient use of taxpayers' resources as well as to distortions in resource allocation. Generous corporate tax incentives, aside from possibly generating tax revenue displacement effects across regions through plant and employment shifts, may be viewed as a form of state aid to industry that distorts competition and resource allocation. This is of particular relevance for the special corporate tax credit granted for fixed-asset investments above ESP 2 500 million. As only big companies may be able to carry out such sizeable investments, it might be argued that such incentives are discriminatory and distort competition against companies that do not receive such aids. On these grounds, the European Commission has referred the case of the investment by the Korean multinational Daewoo to the European Court, stating that it was granted illegitimate *ad hoc* state aid in the form of special tax incentives. This enterprise might hence be requested to refund the 45 per cent special tax credit it had been granted to build a refrigerator plant in Vitoria. On the other hand, the more generous tax subsidies granted for environmental expenses and staff training are of a generic nature, well focused, and could help companies internalise the externalities arising from these activities.

Preferential tax regimes aimed at financial and related services

Moreover, the Basque Country and Navarra operate potentially preferential headquarters tax regimes (the Basque and Navarra Co-ordination Centre regimes), targeting "Management, Co-ordination and Financial" activities of international corporate groups. Companies qualifying for this special corporate income tax regime may choose to assess taxable income according to the general method (based on their accounting profit) or according to the simplified method (25 per cent share of their non-financial expenses). The Basque Country and Navarra headquarters regimes potentially discriminate against domestic profit taxation (being hence of concern for horizontal equity), while the assessment of taxable income on the basis of non-financial expenses may be less transparent. The Basque and Navarra co-ordination centres are being examined by the Spanish courts. Therefore, a verdict in domestic courts is expected. A holding company regime (ETVE) also applies in Spain to all foreign equities holding companies. Dividends paid to and capital gains realised from the sale of shares by qualifying entities are exempt from tax provided that: *a*) the qualifying entities manage for at least one year 5 per cent or more of direct or indirect participation in non-resident companies; *b*) the income of the non-resident company has been subject to a tax identical or analogous to the corporate tax in Spain; and *c*) the dividends or capital gains received do not relate to income of a passive character. The ETVE holding company regime seems consistent with the domestic corporate tax regime. Since these schemes may potentially have international ramifications, they are currently being examined by the OECD Committee on Fiscal Affairs under the recently adopted Guidelines for Dealing with Harmful Preferential Tax Regimes in the OECD Member Countries (see Box 7 below).

Income redistribution and the tax system

Up to 1998, the top marginal rate of the personal income tax in Spain was 56 per cent, among the highest in the OECD. This has, however, not translated into massive income redistribution, as the effective income tax rate did not increase faster along the income scale than in most other OECD countries (Figure 29, panel A). Progressivity is reduced by the vast set of tax allowances and credits, some of which benefit mostly higher income groups.[117] Specifically, tax credits for owner-occupied housing and health expenses – which accounted for 17.1 and 6.6 per cent respectively of total personal income tax expenditures in 1996 – were rising rapidly with income (Figure 30). Tax exemptions and reduced rates on capital income, which benefit mainly high-income groups, further weakened the progressivity of the personal income tax and created horizontal inequities. The reportedly low degree of tax evasion on wage income compared with other income sources may have reinforced this distortion. In fact, while wages and pensions accounted for 61 per cent of household disposable income in 1996, they represented 79 per cent of the personal income tax liabilities.[118]

Despite a decline in top marginal rates, the 1998 personal income tax reform is likely to raise progressivity. Official estimates suggest that the overall tax burden will be cut by 11 per cent, and benefit mostly lower income groups: taxpayers with an annual income of less than ESP 2 million should see their final tax liabilities cut by almost one third (Table 20). This partly reflects the introduction of a progressive tax allowance for labour income, contrasting with the proportional scheme before the reform.[119] The reform also implies a shift of the tax burden from labour to capital as exemptions on capital income have been curtailed. In addition, the reform replaced several tax credits by a tax-exempt living minimum – the *minimo exento*. This has affected the progressivity of the personal income tax in several ways. On the one hand, the tax value of the living minimum grows with the individual's marginal rate and thus benefits mostly higher income groups in absolute terms. On the other hand, some of the tax credits that the living standard minimum has substituted for, were proportional to expenses. As the overall amount was increasing for richer individuals, they also benefited mostly higher income groups. Specifically, taxpayers are no longer granted a tax credit equal to 15 per cent of their health expenditure; the tax-exempt living

Box 7. The OECD's work on harmful tax practices

Globalisation and new electronic technologies can permit a proliferation of tax regimes designed to attract geographically mobile activities. This can occur when discriminatory tax regimes attract investment or savings originating elsewhere and when they facilitate the avoidance of other countries' taxes. To provide co-ordinated action for the elimination of harmful tax practices, the OECD issued in May 1998 the Report on Harmful Tax Competition (OECD, 1998e). The Report created a Forum on Harmful Tax Practices, set forth Guidelines for Dealing with Harmful Preferential Regimes in Member Countries, and adopted a series of Recommendations* for combating harmful tax practices. This work focuses on geographically mobile activities, such as financial and other service activities.

The Forum on Harmful Tax Practices is responsible for undertaking an ongoing evaluation of existing and proposed preferential tax regimes in Member and non-member countries, analysing the effectiveness of counteracting measures, including non-tax measures, and examining whether particular jurisdictions constitute tax havens. The Forum has a one-year time period within which to prepare a list of tax havens, taking into account factors set out in the Tax Competition Report. The main factors are: a) no or low effective tax rates; b) lack of effective exchange of information; c) lack of transparency; and d) absence of a requirement of substantial activities.

The Forum is also co-ordinating a self-review by Member countries of their preferential regimes to determine whether those regimes constitute harmful tax practices. Member countries' measures that constitute harmful tax practices must be reported to the Forum within a two-year time frame. The key factors to be used in identifying and assessing harmful preferential tax regimes are: a) no or low effective tax rates; b) "ring fencing" of regimes; c) lack of transparency; and d) lack of effective exchange of information. The Forum is also working to associate non-member countries with the Guidelines.

The Guidelines on harmful tax practices incorporate a standstill provision, and a roll-back provision. Under the standstill provision, the Member countries are to refrain from: i) adopting new measures; and ii) extending the scope of or strengthening existing measures, that constitute harmful tax practices.

Under the roll-back provision, the harmful features of preferential regimes must be eliminated before the end of five years. The Guidelines also provide that the Forum should be used by Member countries to co-ordinate their national and treaty responses to harmful tax practices.

The Forum on Harmful Tax Practices is exploring the possibility of a wider mandate and also is assisting with work on other topics that may be relevant to the subject of harmful tax practices. These topics include, among others: restricting the deductibility of payments made to tax haven entities; imposing withholding taxes on payments to residents of countries with harmful preferential regimes; the application of transfer pricing rules and guidelines; and financial innovation issues.

---

* Luxembourg and Switzerland abstained, and will not be bound in any manner by the Report or OECD Recommendations in this area.

Figure 29. **International comparisons of average personal income tax rates and total tax wedges**

1998, by multiples of APW taxable income

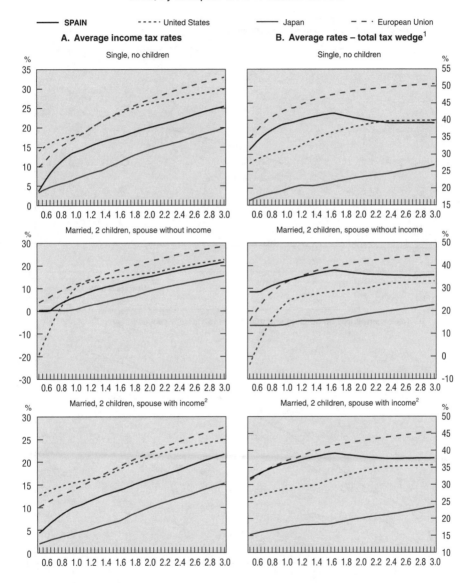

1. Income tax plus employers and employees social security contributions, less cash benefits.
2. Spouse earning 0.67 per cent of the income of the Average Production Worker.
Source: OECD, *The Tax/Benefit Position of Employees.*

Figure 30. **Progressivity of the personal income tax**
1996

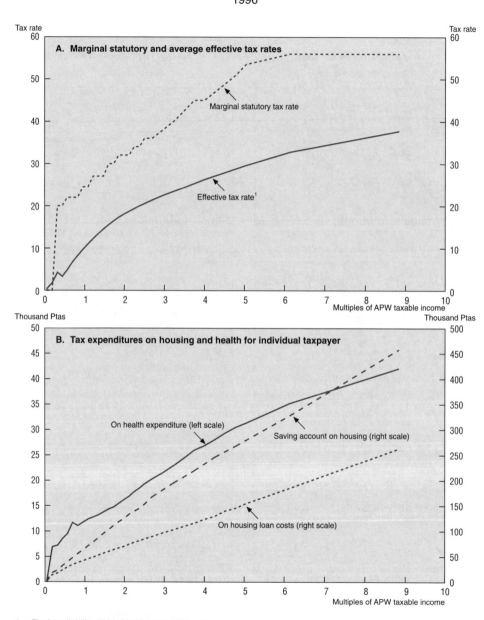

1. Final tax liability divided by the taxable income.
Source: Ministry of Economy and Finance.

Table 20. **Cut in the tax burden: estimated impact of the 1998
personal income tax reform**

By level of income

	Taxpayers (as a percentage of total taxpayers)	Cut in personal income tax liabilities (percentage)
Less than ESP 2 million	60.3	29.7
More than ESP 2 million and less than ESP 3 million	19.8	15.0
More than ESP 3 million and less than ESP 5 million	14.3	8.3
More than ESP 5 million	5.6	6.2
Total	**100.0**	**11.1**

Source: Ministerio de Economía y Hacienda (1998), *Memoria Económica del Anteproyecto de ley de Reforma del IRPF.*

standard minimum is supposed to cover a standard amount of health expenditure.[120] Furthermore, the reform has introduced a ceiling on tax credits for expenses related to owner-occupied housing, which tends to increase for richer individuals. As a side effect, streamlining deductions as well as cutting marginal statutory rates for the most affluent income groups could reduce avoidance, and thus increase the actual progressivity of the system (high-income earners typically have better access to avoidance instruments, *e.g.* by shifting income into foreign countries with low taxes).

Income distribution is also affected by the financing rules and the associated transfers of the social security system.[121] Family benefits, for instance, are tax-exempt but are means-tested. Drastically flattening total tax schedules are the floors and ceilings on social security contributions.[122] Floors penalise low-income wage earners. And, contrasting with most other OECD countries, the overall tax burden decreases for incomes above 1.5 times the average wage (Figure 29, panel B) reflecting social security ceilings. Another channel of redistribution is the taxation of consumption. In order to introduce some progressivity into the VAT system, Spain has one reduced VAT rate and a super-reduced rate – 7 and 4 per cent respectively – while its standard rate is below that of most EU countries.[123] However, international evidence suggests that reduced rates may not support redistribution since higher income levels could benefit most in absolute terms because they consume more of all goods and services.[124] This is particularly true for expenses on restaurants and hotels, as well as health, which typically rise with the level of income but are taxed in Spain at reduced VAT rates. An important issue is who finally bears the tax burden. Taxes levied on a given base may end up being shifted along the production and distribution chain depending on the degree of competition in labour and product markets. Tax shifting is difficult to assess but one may reasonably argue that taxes can less easily be shifted onto mobile sources, *i.e.* highly qualified labour and capital. Low-qualified, low-paid labour would thus bear most of the taxes.

Fiscal federalism

The Basque country and Navarra regions already have extensive spending and revenue raising powers

Spending and revenue raising powers vary significantly across the 17 regional governments. At one extreme are the Basque country and the Navarra region. These two regions now have their own personal and corporate income tax systems and collect most taxes. Most expenditure powers have been devolved, a main exception being social security transfers (excluding health) which are implemented by Spain's unitary social security system. For other spending programmes carried out exclusively at the State level (mainly foreign affairs, defence and some network infrastructure), these two regions pay a share to the State, the *"cupo"* (Box 8). Under this financing model, transfers across regions are thus limited to social security transfers and contributions, and to the participation in spending associated with defence, foreign affairs and some network infrastructure.

Extending this model to other regions would require to reconsider transfers across regions

Revenue raising powers of the other regional governments are more limited. In 1997, these so-called "common regime" regions were granted revenue-raising powers on a share of the personal income tax and on the so-called "ceded" taxes (mainly on property and property transfers).[125] Taxes over which the common regime regions have revenue raising powers account for about one fifth and one half of their total and unconditional resources, respectively (Box 9). The remaining tax receipts are pooled at the central government level and redistributed across regions so as to guarantee each region the ability to provide a given standard of public services. Through this redistribution of tax receipts, rich regions contribute to the finances of the poorest regions. They would thus benefit most if the Basque country model were extended to them. However, extending this system to the rest of Spain would entail to reconsider two principles embodied in the Constitution: solidarity across regions and sufficiency in resources to finance the activities transferred to each of them.

Enhanced reliance on the regions' own personal income tax receipts induces a high volatility of resources

The implementation of the 1997-2001 financing system for the common regime regions implies that a larger proportion of a region's financial resources depends directly upon that region's economic performance. Specifically, for a region which accepted the agreement, the share of unconditional financial

Box 8. **The economic agreement between the Spanish State and the Basque Country**

Financial flows from the Basque Country to the Central government

Financial relations between the State and the Basque Country are shaped by a transfer, called "*cupo*". It flows from the region to the central government, very similar to the funding of EU common policies but contrasting with the model prevailing in most other OECD countries whereby financial transfers flow from the higher to lower authorities. A major reason for these peculiar arrangements is history. A similar system was in force from the end of the nineteenth century to the civil war. It was abolished in 1937 in two of the three Basque provinces because they were then considered as traitors to the Franco regime. The *cupo* corresponds to the Basque Country's contributions to the expenses which are borne by the State (mainly foreign affairs and defence-related expenditures, and some infrastructure investment programmes such as airports and ports). Since the amount of the *cupo* depends on expenditure decisions taken by the State, some observers describe this system as one of "unilateral risk" falling on the regional government, contrary to most existing models of fiscal federalism where the State bears most of the risks.* The Basque Country's contribution to expenditures at the State level is defined by the ratio of the regional GDP to the national GDP (for the period 1997-2001, the Basque Country's share has been set at 6.24 per cent).

Large responsibilities in setting and in collecting taxes

The Basque Country is responsible for setting the conditions, managing, inspecting and collecting all taxes, except for custom duties and some excise taxes (VAT rates and exemptions are set by the central government but collected by the Basque tax administration).

Most prominent tax incentives in the Basque Country and Navarra special corporate tax regimes are: *a*) a reduction in taxable profits during the first 4 years of profitable operation – by 99, 75, 50 and 25 per cent respectively (50 per cent in the case of Navarra); *b*) a general tax credit (15 per cent) granted for investment in new fixed assets – increased by an extra 5 per cent where there is concomitant employment creation; *c*) a special tax credit of 45 per cent granted for fixed investment above ESP 2 500 millions; *d*) more generous tax credits (30 per cent) for investment in R&D, as well as for expenses on staff training and on environmental improvement; and *e*) a reduced statutory corporate tax rate of 32.5 per cent, and *f*) carry-forward of tax losses over a longer period (15 instead of 10 years).

The personal income tax system differs also significantly from elsewhere in Spain. The tax schedule is more progressive (marginal rates ranging from 17 to 50 per cent – compared with a 18 to 48 per cent range in the rest of Spain), and tax credits covering family expenses have not been substituted by a family exempted income.

---

* See Lambarri, C. and van Mourik, A. (1998).

Box 9. **The financing of regional governments under the so-called common regime**

In addition to conditional State transfers earmarked for specific purposes (the largest being social security transfers), regional governments' financial resources include:

- Taxes whose administration was already transferred to the regional governments in 1997 (taxes on wealth, inheritances and donations, property transactions, stamp duties and gambling). These taxes accounted, on average, for 23.3 per cent of the regions' unconditional resources in 1996.
- User fees and charges for the services they provided. Related revenues account for 2.4 per cent of the regions' unconditional resources.
- A 15 per cent share of total personal income tax revenues collected in their jurisdiction and over which they do not have any taxing powers.[1]
- From 1997, an additional 15 per cent share of total personal income tax revenues collected in their jurisdiction. The 12 regions which have accepted the 1997-2001 financing model have gained the right to set rates and deductions, within some limits. This component accounts on average for less than one fourth of the regions' unconditional resources, though with significant variations from one to another region (from almost 60 per cent in Madrid to 12 per cent for Galicia, see Figure 31), largely reflecting differences in per capita income and competencies transferred.
- A given share of overall tax revenues collected by the State (the so-called *Participación en los Ingresos del Estado*, PIE), including all direct and indirect taxes, and social security contributions.

In the 1992-96 financing model, the total amount of unconditional resources made available to the regional governments was determined on the basis of the estimated cost of activities taken over by the regional governments. The main variables used for the estimation and the distribution of resources across regions were: "distributive variables" (population, geographic and administrative dispersion), and "redistributive variables" (mainly income per capita). The closing variable of this financing model was the share of the State tax revenues – revised every 5 years – which was allocated between regions so as to guarantee each region the ability to provide a given standard of public services. Sharing the overall tax revenues collected by the State was thus the main mechanism for implementing inter-regional solidarity transfers. The increase in the regions' unconditional resources over the five-year period was the result of both the tax performance in their jurisdictions (for the three first components of their unconditional resources) and in the overall Spanish territory (through the share in State tax revenues). Three regions (Andalucía, Castilla La Mancha and Extremadura), which have not accepted the 1997-2001 financing model, continue to be financed under these conditions, though without adjustment in the total amount of unconditional transfers allocated to them to reflect changes in distributive and redistributive variables. These regions do not have any taxing powers either on the so-called ceded taxes or on the regional component of the personal income tax.

The 1997-2001 financing model for 12 out of the 15 common regime regions has changed the rationale of the system, by replacing the implicit redistribution scheme between regions by two explicit guarantees on each region's financial resources.[2] *First*,

(*continued on next page*)

(continued)

the so-called "State revenue share" will increase in line with national GDP, from the 1996 reference year and no longer in line with tax revenues. The guarantee scheme means that if tax revenues at the national level grow less than national income, regional resources will not be affected. The State will have to bear the brunt of adjustment cost. *Second*, if personal income tax revenues collected in a region's jurisdiction, and devolved to it, grow less than the national GDP, the State is committed to proceed with a compensating transfer. If it were to grow more than the national GDP, the region keeps the extra-revenues, thus limiting the scope of the implicit redistribution across regions.

---

1. Regional governments were deemed to gain taxing powers over this share when all of them have assumed the responsibility over the education system. This might not happen before the end of 2001. A few regional governments, for instance, the autonomous community of Madrid, have not been granted this share; their resource level would have exceeded the overall amount of unconditional resources required to undertake the activities transferred to them.
2. The model has been designed to be revenue neutral using 1996 as a base year. The total amount of unconditional resources allocated to each region has not been adjusted for distributive and redistributive variables. In particular, those regions where population growth has been rapid may be penalised.

---

resources that depends on its own personal income tax doubled. It varies nevertheless significantly from one region to another (Figure 31), and is higher in the richest regions. However, the poorest regions, whose income is expected to grow on average faster than the richest ones, should benefit most over the medium term. The implementation of the agreement could result in an increased volatility of the regional tax base and a wide dispersion in the degree of revenue risks across regions. Reinforcing the associated risk for the regions' revenues is the volatility of the household income tax base, which is much higher than for private consumption or nominal GDP (Table 21). Furthermore, the volatility in personal income tax revenues is substantially higher in small regions with little industrial diversification. The standard deviation of Castilla La Mancha or Extremadura's personal income tax is, for instance, much higher than the national average.

Tax competition across regions, allowed for by the new financing system, could also induce a further increase in the variability of the regions' resources. However, to prevent tax-induced migration flows across regions, measures were introduced to limit the taxing powers of regional governments (imposing bands on tax rates) and a stricter definition of tax residence was implemented. So far, none of the regional governments has changed marginal rates on the regional component of the personal income tax though many of them have introduced or increased deductions associated with family or housing expenses. This may partly

Figure 31. **The financing of the regional governments**
1996

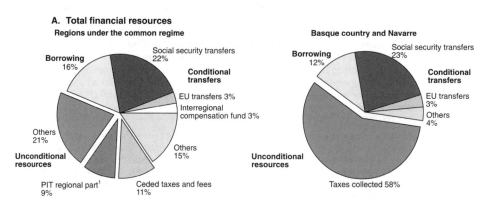

A. **Total financial resources**

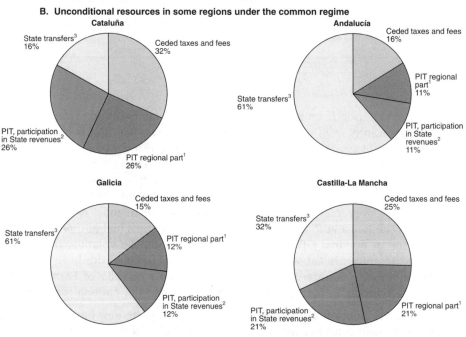

B. **Unconditional resources in some regions under the common regime**

1. Corresponds to the 15 per cent of personal income tax revenue collected in the region, over which those regions which accepted the 1997-2001 financing model have gained taxing powers since 1997.
2. Corresponds to the additional share (for most regions, 15 per cent) of the personal income tax revenues collected in their juridiction and over which they cannot modify the marginal rates or deductions.
3. Corresponds to the regional share of overall tax revenues collected by the State.

Source: Bank of Spain, Agencia Tributaria.

Table 21. **Volatility of tax bases and revenues at national and regional levels**

	GDP[1] 1986-96		Private consumption		Household income (before tax) 1986-95		Indirect taxes 1986-96		Personal income tax 1990-96		GDP per capita 1995 Spain = 100
	Average growth rate	Standard deviation	Average growth rate 1986-96	Standard deviation 1992-96	Average growth rate	Standard deviation	Average growth rate	Standard deviation	Average growth rate	Standard deviation	
At national level	**8.6**	**3.0**	**8.4**	**1.4**	**9.3**	**3.5**	**8.2**	**5.0**	**6.8**	**3.2**	**100.0**
At a regional level											
Andalucía	8.5	3.8	8.4	2.1	9.4	3.8	n.a.	n.a.	6.9	3.5	74.3
Aragón	8.1	3.3	7.9	1.6	9.0	3.8	n.a.	n.a.	6.1	3.8	113.8
Asturias	7.0	2.5	7.6	1.5	8.0	4.0	n.a.	n.a.	6.5	2.9	91.3
Baleares	8.8	2.8	7.9	1.1	9.4	3.4	n.a.	n.a.	8.1	1.9	136.8
Canarias	8.9	2.8	8.8	1.6	9.6	3.2	n.a.	n.a.	8.9	2.3	92.8
Cantabria	8.4	4.0	8.4	1.8	8.3	3.7	n.a.	n.a.	5.6	2.5	97.2
Castilla y León	7.8	2.0	7.7	1.5	8.5	3.4	n.a.	n.a.	7.3	4.0	90.9
Castilla-La Mancha	8.9	4.1	8.4	1.4	9.2	3.9	n.a.	n.a.	8.4	5.1	82.2
Cataluña	9.2	3.3	8.7	1.4	10.2	4.5	n.a.	n.a.	6.5	3.7	124.6
Ceuta y Melilla	9.1	4.2	8.2	0.8	8.6	3.5	n.a.	n.a.	..	..	..
Extremadura	8.5	3.9	8.1	1.4	9.5	4.0	n.a.	n.a.	9.1	5.4	69.8
Galicia	8.2	2.4	8.0	1.4	8.9	3.7	n.a.	n.a.	8.5	3.2	77.7
Madrid	9.1	3.1	8.2	1.5	9.6	4.5	n.a.	n.a.	5.8	4.1	124.0
Murcia	8.1	3.9	9.5	1.9	8.8	3.9	n.a.	n.a.	7.7	2.7	88.8
Navarra	8.4	4.5	9.6	1.6	10.0	4.2	n.a.	n.a.	..	..	120.9
País Vasco	7.5	2.9	8.0	1.5	8.2	3.8	n.a.	n.a.	..	..	118.1
La Rioja	8.5	3.4	8.7	1.9	9.1	3.7	n.a.	n.a.	7.2	2.0	114.4
Comunidad Valenciana	8.2	3.2	8.1	1.9	9.5	3.9	n.a.	n.a.	7.6	1.6	98.9
Memorandum item:											
At national level, 1986-96	8.6	3.0	8.4	3.1	8.9	3.6	8.2	5.0	13.1	11.5	..

1. Value added data are used for the regions since GDP data are available only for a shorter period.
Source: INE, Agencia Estatal de Administración Tributaria and OECD Secretariat calculations.

reflect the difficulties in estimating the potential revenue impact of any changes in marginal rates, while the costs of introducing tax credits according to the family situation of taxpayers are much easier to assess. Long delays in publishing data on regional personal income tax collection further reinforce this uncertainty and hinder the use of revenue raising powers by the regions (data for the 1997 personal income tax outcome on a regional basis were not made public before July 1999).

The associated revenue guarantee scheme may hinder fiscal consolidation

Aiming to protect the regions against temporary revenue shortfalls, a guarantee scheme was designed in 1996, but amendments in 1998 significantly diminished the degree of fiscal co-responsibility of the regions. In the original agreement, the State committed to partly compensate a region with transfers in the event its personal income tax collection grows more slowly than at the State level.[126] Recognising the increased volatility of the regions' resources which could result from the implementation of the new financing system, the agreement was modified in April 1998, retroactively. From 1997, regional governments no longer face any downside risk on their core financial resources: the State is committed to grant matching transfers to each individual region if the 30 per cent share of personal income tax revenues collected in its jurisdiction or the so-called "share of the State revenues" grows less than nominal GDP.

Such a guarantee scheme poses several problems. First, it is asymmetric since the central government has to pay in the event of bad outcomes while regional governments do not fund an insurance system in the event of good outcomes.[127] It may thus imply a significant cost for the State budget, though difficult to measure since data on the income tax collected by regions are made public with a long delay.[128] In 1997, personal income tax receipts grew less than the national GDP in 14 out of the 15 common regime regions while other tax receipts were booming. The regions thus received compensating transfers for the loss in personal income tax receipts and simultaneously kept the windfall increase in other tax revenues. Overall, additional resources transferred by the State to the regions as a result of the new financing system would amount to around ESP 90 billion (equivalent to 0.5 per cent of the State tax revenues in 1997) had the system been in place for all the common regime regions.[129] Second, guarantees do not provide regional governments with the right incentives to contain expenditures. This will thus make it more difficult to foster fiscal consolidation. Third, the guarantee scheme also constrains efforts to reduce the overall tax burden since the cost would have to be borne exclusively by the central government – as has happened with the personal income tax reform.[130] However, the low income tax revenue elasticity experienced since the early 1990s, combined with highly income-elastic outlays devolved to the regions (e.g. health, or to a lesser extend education), may induce fiscal imbalances as real income grows that might partly justify these guarantees.

Issues of tax competition stemming from broadening the existing model of special corporate tax regimes

Tax competition between lower levels of government may be a healthy feature of the tax system, enhancing its efficiency, as long as it does not erode tax bases to such an extent that this would lead to the underprovision of public goods. At present, corporate income tax revenues – other than those collected in the Basque Country and Navarra – are pooled nation-wide and, furthermore, companies with fiscal residence in the Basque Country but nation-wide operations are subject to the common regime (Box 10). More generous corporate income taxation and tax incentives for investment provided by the Basque Country regime might involve, first, shifts of the corporate income tax base – and hence revenue effects for government budgets. Second, they could induce shifts in plant location and employment that involve real resource reallocation and generate further revenue effects. Current arrangements are not likely to involve such shifts within Spain for companies below the ESP 500 million threshold, as tax incentives are granted according to fiscal residence – independently of operations or plant location.

Box 10.   **Sharing corporate income tax revenues between the Basque Country and the central government**

Companies qualifying for the Basque Country corporate income tax must set their fiscal residence in one of its territories and realise at least 25 per cent of the turnover within their borders. Companies with fiscal residence in the Basque Country, with turnover falling short of this threshold, are subject to the general regime. Corporate income tax liabilities determined according to each of the two regimes are assigned to each jurisdiction (the central government or the Basque Country) according to the following rules:*

   a) Companies with turnover below 500 million pesetas are liable only to the jurisdiction of their fiscal residence – whichever the place they operate.
   b) Corporate income tax liabilities of companies with turnover above 500 million pesetas are assigned to the Basque Country if they operate exclusively in its area, independently of fiscal residence.
   c) Corporate income tax liabilities of companies with turnover exceeding 500 million pesetas that operate in both territories are shared – according to relative operations ascertained under VAT regulations – wherever the companies' fiscal residence.

---

* See, Basque Government (1998), art. 17 to 20.

Tax-induced location shifts might, nevertheless, arise for companies above the ESP 500 million turnover threshold, in order to benefit from the more generous corporate tax provisions in the Basque Country special regime – particularly those granted for general investment purposes and business start-ups. A case in point, which the European Commission has been investigating on the grounds of distortions to the single market, concerns the tax subsidies received by the enterprise *Ramodin*. This firm shifted its fiscal residence to the Basque Country district of Laguardia (Alava), from the neighbouring district of Logroño, in order to benefit from the special corporate tax credits for investment provided by the Basque Country special regime. Fiscal residence shifts could deprive some regions of corporate income tax revenues to the benefit of regions offering more attractive regimes. Although existing corporate tax-sharing agreements may mute revenue effects, location shifts will involve changes in resource allocation, as well as revenue effects stemming from other taxable bases (personal income tax, indirect taxes).

Local governments: heavy reliance on taxes and licensing fees on land and real estate

The high dependency of local authorities' resources on land values tends – in conjunction with long administrative procedures to requalify the potential use of land – to drive prices up. In 1997, 42 per cent of current revenues raised by local authorities originated from taxes on land and real estate (22 per cent of their total revenues).[131] Since then, a new State Land Regime and Valuation Law was approved (June 1998).[132] Its main objective of lowering land prices has not been achieved so far – prices have continued to rise steeply, by over 50 per cent for public land auctioned over the 12-month period following the reform. This development partly reflects the absence of alternative revenue sources for local authorities, giving them an incentive to restrict land supply in order to drive prices up and thus boost their revenues. On the other hand, local authorities' revenues from user fees and charges on specific services contribute a relatively low share of their resources, partly owing to the inadequacy of the law in stipulating over which goods and services these fees and charges could be levied, unclear responsibility for collection and lax enforcement (Petitbó and Povedano, 1998; Moreno, 1998; and Echebarría, 1998). The case of wastewater fees is revealing in this regard since municipalities are responsible for wastewater treatment.

Taxes to achieve environmental goals: the case of wastewater and energy

Largely reflecting low prices, pressures on available water are among the highest in the OECD. However, a large amount of industrial and, in particular, agricultural effluents receives little or no treatment (see OECD,1997e). The 1985 Water Act states that industrial and municipal discharge permit holders must pay a water pollution fee – *canon de vertido*. The fee was established to fund wastewater treatment facilities, though its level seems unrealistically low (Castillo Lopez, 1999). The proceeds can be shared *de facto* between the three levels of governments while responsibilities for building and managing these facilities are spread between several public entities and government levels, cutting the link between the fee and service provision. As a matter of fact, many industries have refused to pay, arguing that the investment plan for the associated treatment plants were not approved – 40 per cent of the levies for authorised dischargers were not paid in 1997. Furthermore, the fee is imposed only on holders of discharge permits while a large proportion of discharges was still carried out without a permit (80 per cent), partly reflecting complex permitting procedures and enforcement problems.[133] In addition, water used for irrigation is exempted from wastewater charges despite its significant pollution potential of ground and surface water resources associated with a generally intensive use of pesticides and fertilisers. Overall, wastewater charges amounted to only ESP 7 billion in 1997 – *i.e.* 1.3 per cent of the water bill paid by consumers. In addition, water prices often do not fully cover actual delivery costs.[134]

As with water, energy taxation is not well geared towards internalising environmental externalities. In this context, combating climate change by reducing greenhouse gas emissions as agreed in the Kyoto Protocol will probably be a major challenge. In the burden sharing amongst EU countries following the Kyoto Protocol, Spain has been granted a 15 per cent increase in greenhouse gas emissions for the period 1990-2010, while emissions will have to be reduced by 8 per cent for the EU as a whole. However, Spain's CO_2 emissions have already risen by 9.6 per cent between 1990 and 1996 and robust growth since then suggests that the ceiling will be reached quickly.[135] Changes to energy taxation could be part of a strategy to reduce CO_2 emissions. Energy taxation is in general lower in Spain than elsewhere in Europe (Table 22). It is currently not being used

Table 22. **Share of taxes in energy prices**

1998

	Gasoline (premium unleaded)	Diesel	Electricity (household)	Electricity (industry)	Heating oil (household)	Gas (household)	Gas (industry)
Spain	**68.7**	**58.0**	**18.0**	**4.9**	**44.1**	**15.1**	**0.0**
Denmark	72.4	39.5	60.3	17.3	64.2	28.1	C[1]
France	81.2	69.5	28.1	n.a.[1]	43.4	17.1	0.0
Germany	75.2	63.1	13.8	n.a.[1]	33.4	18.8	12.7
Italy	74.7	65.2	26.5	17.5	72.0	43.3	9.7
Portugal	72.8	57.7	4.8	0.0	59.9	X[1]	n.a.[1]
United Kingdom	81.4	78.6	4.8	0.0	26.9	4.8	0.0

1.   X: not applicable; C: price is confidential; n.a.: not available.
Source: IEA, *Energy Prices and Taxes* (OECD).

to promote consumption of cleaner fuels,[136] but taxation is primarily driven by the need to raise government revenues. In a first step, energy taxation could be restructured to reflect the carbon content of the various fuels, for instance, coal be more heavily taxed and gas more lightly. Fuel switching would reduce emissions. If that were not sufficient the carbon tax may have to be raised to induce further reductions. A climate change policy should be more comprehensive, though, and evaluate all the available options. Those would include a review of the moratorium concerning the building of nuclear power plants. Moreover, all greenhouse gases should be covered by the strategy, emission trading may be more attractive than taxation, and the flexibility mechanism allowed for in the Kyoto Protocol may provide attractive solutions, if abatement cost are lower elsewhere.

Main options for reform

The tax system has been designed to achieve a large number of objectives, which may conflict with one another. Reforming the tax system thus requires deciding which objectives are the most important and how far they should be pursued by the tax system or by other policies. Nevertheless, to take advantage of policy complementarities and improve the effectiveness of tax policy instrument assignments, further reform of the tax system would need to proceed in tandem with labour market and social security reforms. In addition, designing a comprehensive tax reform would have a stronger impact than reforming a limited number of taxes, because of the interconnection of the various activities of taxpayers. Moreover, taxpayers can transform the legal character of these activities – so as to reduce their tax burden – without affecting their economic content. Main tax reform options involve: *i*) Further reducing the tax burden on labour, with priority given to the low-paid, by shifting towards taxation of consumption; *ii*) Promoting tax neutrality across savings instruments and corporate tax regimes, and enhancing the effectiveness of tax incentives to investment. Improved tax neutrality would also promote tax equity, broaden the tax base and enhance tax compliance. *iii*) Strengthening tax decentralisation – also with a view to complying effectively with the Stability and Growth Pact – by: *a*) reinforcing incentives to match regional spending by locally raised tax revenues; and *b*) providing the right incentives for a sound management of public finance at the regional and central level. This section sets out the main options along these lines for reforming the tax system. They are summarised by main tax in Box 11.

Reconsider the cost-effectiveness of existing tax preferences **versus** *structural reforms*

Some of the objectives pursued through differentiated tax treatments could be more efficiently handled through other policies. The highly progressive

---

Box 11. Synopsis of options for reforming the tax system

Further reform the personal income tax

- *Further streamline tax expenditures to reduce distortions and broaden the tax base.* Aim at symmetry in the tax treatment of unemployment benefits and severance payments to reduce distortions in the labour market. Tax base broadening would allow to further reduce the tax rates, especially the top tax rates, which are still relatively high by international comparison.
- *Further reduce the preferential tax treatment granted to owner-occupied housing.* Phasing out tax preferences to housing would improve the allocation of saving, improve the distribution of the tax burden, and reduce disincentives to regional labour mobility.
- *Further alleviate the taxation of distributed profits.* This would enhance tax neutrality towards corporate financing and would raise households' participation in the market for risk capital.
- *Promote neutrality concerning financial savings decisions by eliminating differences in capital gains taxation for different holding periods.* Taxing all capital gains at the current flat rate would eliminate financial lock-in effects and improve the allocation of financial savings.
- *Replace the "forfaitaire" system of taxation ("módulos") for the self-employed by an income assessment* based on proper accounting rules, to improve transparency and enhance horizontal equity.

Further reform the corporate income tax

- *Implement a flat corporate tax rate.* This would improve corporate tax neutrality, encourage risk taking and eliminate opportunities for tax avoidance.
- *Balance tax incentives to intangible capital investment,* by raising the tax credit for staff training. This would reinforce the effectiveness of tax incentives granted to investment in R&D, which are very generous in international comparison. It would, furthermore, support labour market reform efforts.
- *Further improve provisions for carrying forward and backward losses.* This would smooth tax liabilities and enhance incentives for risk taking.
- *Phase out ad hoc tax incentives – especially those targeted according to investment size – in the Basque Country and Navarra corporate tax regimes* as they might distort competition. They should be replaced by a more neutral tax scheme, aiming to encourage risk taking. Bring in line the Basque Country foreign security holding company regime with the general regime. It is less transparent than the general regime, is very generous, and may give rise to tax avoidance.

Enhance tax administration and tax compliance

- *Assign more resources to reducing tax evasion.* Improve the use of property information and increase resources dedicated to the detection of undeclared activities. Enhancing tax enforcement will improve the distribution of the personal income tax burden.

(continued on next page)

(continued)

Adjust the tax mix

- *Reduce rates of social security contributions on the low-income range by lifting rate ceilings, while abolishing contribution floors.* This would help rebalance the distribution of the tax burden on labour, and would improve employment prospects of low-skilled workers.
- *Reduce the tax burden on labour.* To finance revenue shortfalls, the priority should be given to expenditure cuts. As a second best, a switch to indirect taxes could be envisaged.
- *Apply more consistently the "benefit principle" on a wider range of publicly provided services.* This would provide a better link between private benefits and social costs. Increasing and better enforcing waste water pollution fees, for instance, would help both improve scarce water resource management and achieve environmental goals.
- *Consider taxing pollutants according to their environmental costs* in order to provide the right market signals to consumers and producers. To reduce greenhouse gas emissions, energy taxation should reflect the carbon content of the various fuels.

Enhance tax decentralisation

- *Match rising regional expenditure competencies by increased reliance on locally raised taxes,* rather than on transfers from central government. Greater tax decentralisation would give a better incentive to regions to grow their tax base and control expenditure, fostering fiscal consolidation at the national level.
- *A further devolution of taxing powers to the regions should rely on a wider basket of taxes.* This would reduce the volatility of regional tax revenues and the potential costs of guarantees for the central government. A tax-sharing arrangement on the less volatile VAT could be envisaged.
- *Assign to municipalities a broader tax bundle (especially excises and user fees),* to reduce their reliance on land and real estate taxes that hinder urban land development. The urban land appreciation tax is most harmful in this regard and should be amended.

---

schedule of the personal income tax distorts economic decisions while tax reliefs have been used to pursue diverse social and economic goals: *e.g.* promoting housing, health, saving, SMEs and employment. However, most tax reliefs have had questionable impacts on income redistribution either because they cannot benefit the most needy (whose income is below the minimum taxable income) or because they increase the richer an individual is. In this regard, the cost-effectiveness of preferential tax treatments granted to housing, health, and leisure expenses should be reassessed. Expenditure programmes could achieve distributional objectives better. Better targeted, they are much less costly for the budget. Likewise, the reduced corporate tax rate for SMEs has been granted, partly, to compensate for higher financing and administrative costs. Tackling these impediments, in particular through an acceleration of the ongoing process to simplify administrative requirements, should become a priority. The social security system combines ceilings and floors on contributions and a complex system of reduced contribution rates on hiring several vulnerable groups of workers on a new permanent contract. These two features have raised non-wage labour costs for low-paid wage earners, and they should be re-examined. Streamlining tax reliefs which create labour market segmentation, and phasing out of ceilings and floors, combined with a labour market reform (in particular employment protection measures), could contribute more decisively to sustain the Spanish economy's employment performance. Along the same lines, easing the regulatory constraints on the supply and use of land would be more efficient than the granting of a preferential treatment of owner-occupied housing which is largely capitalised in home prices.

Reduce the tax burden on labour income

Tax policy reforms aiming at improving labour market outcomes would need to be carried out in tandem with labour market reforms, to take advantage of policy complementarities. Cutting social security contributions at the low-end of the pay scale should be a priority. This would reduce the regressive pattern of labour income taxation and improve employment prospects of low-skilled workers who are more vulnerable to the adverse effects of a high tax wedge. Suppressing the minimum social security payment, which is even more penalising for the low skilled, would be of immediate concern. To achieve revenue neutrality, a first possibility consists in lifting social security contribution ceilings. As pensions covered by social security contributions are designed on an income support rather than on an insurance principle, a change in ceilings should not inevitably call for a matching increase in benefit entitlements. Raising the employment rate by reducing the tax wedge on the employed is also needed to enhance the sustainability of the pay-as-you-go social security system in view of ageing population prospects. Though a reduced tax burden on labour should be paid for by cuts in primary expenditure, as a second best, a shift onto other tax bases might also be considered. Raising consumption-based taxes would be a natural possibility, in view of their rather low GDP share compared with other OECD countries and given that consumption's share in GDP is broadly similar to that of the gross wage bill. However, altering the tax mix towards increased taxation of consumption changes income distribution in a way that might need to be taken into account in policy design. Such a tax shift involves higher effective taxation for those on transfer income – especially of unemployed and pensioners. At the same time, reducing social security contributions on the low-paid would help smooth the distributional consequences of a switch to consumption taxes to pay for the projected rise in the social expenditure burden.

Macroeconomic model simulations – carried out by the European Commission using the Quest II model and by the OECD Secretariat using the Interlink model – can help to broadly assess the relative pay-off, in terms of growth and employment, of changes in the tax mix (Table 23; the main properties of the simulations are described in Annex II). A reduction in labour taxes matched by broader social security reform – mirrored in these simulations by reduced government transfers to households – has a much stronger employment and output impact than cuts in labour taxes offset by an increase in other taxes – especially consumption taxes. However, even though the long-run output response to a shift in the tax mix from labour to consumption taxes may seem subdued, the pay off is far from negligible. For instance, raising the effective VAT rate in Spain to the EU average would allow labour taxes to be reduced in a revenue-neutral manner

Table 23. **Long-run effects of tax changes: model-based estimates**[1]

Differences from baseline in per cent

		GDP	Employment
1 per cent of GDP reduction in:[2]			
Labour taxes	**Spain**[3]	**0.80**	**1.00**
	Spain	**0.91**	**0.76**
	EU	2.08	1.83
Corporate income taxes	**Spain**	**2.02**	**0.39**
	EU	3.09	1.06
Consumption-based taxes	**Spain**	**0.66**	**0.54**
	EU	1.46	1.28
1 per cent of GDP shift from:			
Labour to consumption-based taxes	**Spain**	**0.26**	**0.23**
	EU	0.64	0.57
Labour to corporate income taxes	**Spain**	**−1.12**	**0.38**
	EU	−1.04	0.76
Corporate income to consumption-based taxes	**Spain**	**1.35**	**−0.15**
	EU	1.60	−0.22
Tax changes to match projected rise in social security cost resulting from ageing[4]			
Increase in labour taxes	**Spain**	**−2.84**	**−2.48**
	EU	−6.89	−6.00
Increase in consumption-based taxes	**Spain**	**−0.90**	**−0.73**
	EU	−2.03	−1.72

1. Simulations (except for first row) are based on the European Commission's Quest II model.
2. Offset by a reduction in government transfer payments to households.
3. Simulation using the OECD Interlink model.
4. Projected social security expenditures span over the period up to 2030.
Source: European Commission, DG II and OECD Secretariat.

by around 2.5 percentage points of GDP.[137] This could lead to a ⅔ per cent permanent increase in the level of GDP. Moreover, there is considerable room to bring this growth impact closer to the – twice as high – average response in the European Union, by stepping up the ongoing process of labour market reform.

To maximise the employment impact of labour tax cuts, after-tax replacement income should be kept constant in real terms, rather than as a fraction of income from work. If this were not the case, wage moderation and enhanced work incentives stemming from a drop in the tax wedge would be largely muted, leading to a rather weak employment response.[138] Moreover, to remove tax-induced distortions in the labour market and enhance incentives of workers on replacement income to re-enter employment, severance payments should be included in taxable income, as is the case with unemployment benefits since 1994. Tax cuts on personal income should not be reflected in increased after-tax benefits from employment security provisions and unemployment insurance.

A broad window of opportunity for a more ambitious reduction of the tax burden on labour will be provided by the new round of discussions on the *Toledo Pact* in 2000. In the absence of pension reform, a substantial hike in taxation would be called for to offset the projected increase in social security expenditures stemming from population ageing. Simulations by the European Commission, using the Quest II model, have assessed the impact on GDP and employment of two alternative scenarios to match the projected increase in social security cost. *First*, an increase in labour income taxes and, *second*, a wider spreading of the cost by an increase in indirect taxes (Table 23). In Spain, the long-run output and employment costs turn out, in both cases, to be lower than the EU average. It is substantial, however, with a permanent GDP loss of nearly 3 per cent and an employment loss of 2.5 per cent (both assessed over the long term), if labour taxes were to finance the increased expenditure. The cost in terms of foregone output and lost jobs would be considerably lower if, instead, higher social spending were to be paid for by a rise in indirect taxation. The cost remains, however, sizeable and could be lowered only by a far-reaching pension reform.

Improve the neutrality of the tax system

Improve further tax neutrality on savings instruments and enhance firms' financing channels

Improving further the neutrality of taxation on financial assets would increase the liquidity of the Spanish stock market and the efficiency of resource allocation. This would also promote corporate governance and help to diversify the ownership structure of companies, which is of special relevance for recently privatised enterprises, and thus remove one barrier to competition between firms with intertwined interests but in overlapping markets. Progress entails removing the preferential tax treatment on long-term capital gains, by taxing all capital gains at the current flat rate, eliminating thus lock-in effects that hinder the reallocation of funds from mature, slow-growing enterprises to the most innovative ones. Placing the taxation of dividends and retained earnings on a more equal footing would work in the same direction. At the same time, this would lessen the need to rely on overgenerous tax incentives for business start-ups – as for instance in the Basque Country special corporate tax regime. In addition, the preferential treatment granted to life insurance contracts should be reconsidered since it may induce a misallocation of resources at least for two reasons. First, it gives these financial intermediaries an undue competitive advantage over other financial actors. Second, institutional investors tend to weight their portfolio towards general governments' and mature enterprises' securities, at the detriment of risk-taking and newly created firms. One option for more comprehensive reform would be to tax all income from financial assets with the same flat tax rate, following the Nordic countries' model. This involves a trade-off between equity and efficiency. A low flat tax is likely to have a regressive impact. However, with the advent of the single currency, tax competition could raise pressures to align capital income taxation with that of lower-tax countries. A flat tax also has the advantages of lowering collection costs and being neutral for resource allocation.

Improve neutrality of corporate taxation to further enhance business investment, risk-taking and entrepreneurship

Concerns that SMEs might face cost disadvantages have to be balanced against the need to promote tax neutrality. In the case of SMEs the tax system may not be the best way to deliver aid in a cost-effective way since, to benefit from tax incentives, they need to make profits. Hence, if deemed necessary, aid to SMEs would be best delivered through targeted expenditures (OECD, 1994*b*). On this principle, enhancing the cost effectiveness and the consistency of tax incentives to SMEs, granted through the corporate and personal income taxes and the tax on inheritances and gifts, would involve:

- removing the reduction in the corporate tax rate for smaller companies. A flat-rate corporate tax structure would improve tax neutrality, encourage risk taking and reduce incentives for tax avoidance;
- a further liberalisation of provisions for carrying forward and especially backward losses to enhance incentives for risk taking;[139]
- the phasing out of the "forfaitaire" system of taxation, to improve transparency and enhance horizontal equity in the taxation of self-employed and micro-enterprises;
- the further softening and extension to a wider range of descendants, of the provisions of the inheritance tax aiming to prevent the break-up of family businesses – relief of up to 95 per cent of the inheritance tax base for transfer of small businesses to the spouse, children and

adopted descendants. Streamlining the inheritance tax and the associated exemptions would help improve horizontal equity in the transmission of small businesses.[140]

Focus investment tax incentives and special corporate tax regimes better

Enhancing tax incentives to staff training would rebalance incentives to intangible investment and would help firms internalise the full productivity enhancing impact and labour market benefits of their investments. In addition, improved firm training, by better tuning worker skills to firm activities, could strengthen the links of workers to their companies. It might hence reinforce the impact of recent labour market reforms aiming to reduce the pervasiveness of temporary employment contracts. Promoting firm training could thus be seen as providing a form of implicit employment safeguard, and might allow easing the strict employment protection legislation. As far as the productivity of R&D investment increases along with the skills of the firm's staff, more generous tax incentives to training should enhance the effectiveness of the already generous tax subsidies granted to R&D investment. Carry-over of unused tax credits for investment in training could also be increased (currently limited to 5 years, for up to 35 per cent of tax liabilities).

Tax incentives provided by special corporate tax regimes according to the amount of investment may distort competition and lead to efficiency losses. Moreover, *ad hoc* tax incentives that currently exist in special corporate tax regimes should be phased out, though tax competition based on generic rules, well-focused and transparently targeted, should not be discouraged. Banning *ad hoc* tax incentives would help overcome the structural bargaining weakness of lower-level governments which, faced with threats of firms to relocate, might see no alternative than granting a higher level of tax subsidies to keep firms from moving away. On these principles, the generous tax subsidies granted by the Basque Country special corporate tax regime should be replaced with a more neutral scheme. If the policy aim is to enhance risk taking and entrepreneurship, such a scheme could, for instance, take the form of free carry-back and forward of losses and unused tax credits, so as to smooth the inter-temporal stream of company taxes. Moreover, the preferential headquarters tax regime under the Basque Country legislation is less transparent than the general regime, very generous, and should be harmonised with the general regime.

Phase out tax incentives to owner-occupied housing and remove tax distortions in the housing market

More ambitious steps to reduce tax preferences granted to owner-occupied housing would help remove underlying distortions in the allocation of savings and could rebalance the pattern of private investment towards business investment. This would lead to a higher capital/labour ratio that should enhance labour productivity and further improve employment growth prospects. Priority should be given to further reducing the generosity of personal income tax allowances for interest and principal repayment on owner-occupied home mortgages. This would also induce a more even distribution of the personal income tax burden, as these tax privileges are relatively more beneficial to higher-income taxpayers. Phasing out personal income tax preferences granted to home ownership could provide more impetus to the development of the rental housing market. By easing the pressure of demand on highly regulated urban land supply, this should be mirrored by a drop in home prices. Assigning to municipalities a larger tax bundle could usefully match more fundamental housing tax reform, to help reduce their reliance on real estate and land taxes and, at the same time, improve incentives to liberalise urban land development. This would also induce an easing in housing prices as well as a more even distribution of prices across regions – to the extent that differences in real estate taxes are capitalised into home prices. Enhanced development of the housing rental market, lower home prices and levelling out of price differences across regions might enhance the geographic mobility of labour and improve overall labour market adjustment.

Strengthen fiscal decentralisation

Progress towards balanced and efficient fiscal decentralisation entails further closing the gap between sub-national governments' spending and revenue-raising powers and providing them with the ability to tailor the taxes devolved to them to their specific local conditions. The 1997-2001 financing agreement is a step in this direction. Also improving further the land register, in particular updating property values, would help regional and local governments to better tailor property taxes. Regional and local governments' ability to rely more on the "user/polluter pays" principle (e.g. for wastewater treatment or solid waste disposal, broadcasting) should also be enhanced. An optimal setting of user charges reflecting social costs requires the removal of existing legal impediments restricting both the type of goods and services over which such charges could apply and the level of these charges. Simplifying the administrative procedures (e.g. to grant wastewater discharge permits) and raising sub-national governments' enforcement abilities is also needed. Tax decentralisation may also entail further complex tax rules. Thus, in granting taxing powers to the regions, it would be important to avoid a rise in collection and compliance costs and in tax avoidance.

In granting further revenue-raising powers to the regions to match their spending powers, care should be taken that fiscal decentralisation does not hinder sound fiscal management at the national level and allows solidarity across the whole territory. Further devolution of taxes which are also designed to achieve redistributional objectives is problematic since different rates could entail incentives for migration, and virtuous or vicious circles, if levied at a regional level – the rich moving to low-tax regions, thus enabling further cuts in rates there, while the poor would settle in the regions where social services are the most developed. Additional sources of revenues for the regions could come from consumption taxes. A tax-sharing arrangement could be envisaged for the VAT, following the experience of other EU countries (*e.g.* Belgium and Germany). Consumption taxes have the advantage of generating less volatile revenues than income taxes. In any case, if a revenue guarantee scheme for the regions is needed, it should mimic a true risk-pooling, funded, insurance scheme, and provide the regions with the right incentives to develop their tax base and control expenditure. The current guarantee system entails significant contingent costs for the State and may impair sound finances at the national level. Publishing the regions' fiscal balances in a timely and transparent basis, and strengthening the mechanisms to enforce the internal stability pact along the lines discussed in Chapter I, would also be essential.

On efficiency grounds, inter-jurisdictional competition in corporate tax regimes does not necessarily need to be regulated by a higher level of government. Competitive tax bidding by governments to attract businesses – even if it involves geographic externalities – could lead to efficient business location outcomes, provided governments' offers reflect governments' true valuation of the outcomes (Besley and Seabright, 1999). Regulating inter-jurisdictional tax incentives would thus not necessarily result in better resource allocation, though it might help achieve the same outcome with a lower overall amount of tax subsidies to firms. This might be particularly welcome when governments are subject to hard budget constraints that restrict their ability to spend – as the new financing scheme for the "Autonomous Communities" needs to ensure. Should parts of the corporate income tax be transferred to the regions in the future (as for instance in the United States or in Canada), tax incentives – that may legitimately differ across jurisdictions – would need to be generic and focused on specific targets. In fact, subsidising through tax incentives the private provision of public goods (training, environment upgrading) according to their geographic scarcity does not distort competition. However, to increase transparency and prevent market distortions arising from *ad hoc* tax incentives, a certain degree of harmonisation in the definition of the corporate tax base should be sought, while allowing competition in setting a part of the corporate income tax rate, which should apply to all resident companies.

Notes

1. About 40 and 20 per cent of bank loans to non-financial corporations have a maturity over 5 years and between 1 and 5 years, respectively.

2. The previous Survey and Chapter II of this report present the 1997 labour market reform.

3. The replacement rule for civil servants will be eased at the local level in 2000.

4. A back-of-the-envelope calculation suggests that, with employment growing at 3 per cent, if two thirds of new employees have a productivity level equal to 80 per cent of the average "old" workers, overall productivity growth would be 0.4 percentage points lower.

5. The change in the labour force survey (EPA) methodology in the first quarter of 1999 may also have shifted the unemployment rate downwards (see Box 1).

6. The large share of fixed-term contracts in gross job creation – compared to the 33 per cent share of fixed-term jobs in total employment – reflects the high turnover rate of fixed-term jobs.

7. The CPI reference basket of goods and services is currently based on the 1991 household consumption survey; telecommunications accounted for 1.4 per cent of the consumption basket. Since then, the weight of telecommunication services has increased significantly. Furthermore, the CPI only reflects general offers maintained for at least several months and the rates of new suppliers are only taken into account after a year in the market. For these reasons, telephone prices in the CPI may overstate the actual price charged. Ruiz-Castillo *et al.* (1999), for instance, estimated that the current CPI overstates inflation by 0.6 percentage points when taking into account the biases identified in the Boskin report. The National Statistical Institute (INE) intends to introduce in 2000 a new consumer price index basket based on a more recent household consumption survey. This will probably entail a higher weight of services, some of which are more inflation-prone (*e.g.* restaurants and hotels). Thus, the overall result is uncertain.

8. It is noteworthy that the share of firms and households in the net change in the total liabilities of the non-financial domestic sector rose to 80 per cent on average in 1997-98 from only 35 per cent in 1992-95.

9. However, stronger-than-expected VAT revenues may also partly reflect underestimation of consumption growth, which could in turn account for the slow recorded productivity growth in the current upturn (Box 1).

10. On an accrual basis, up to October 1999, personal income tax revenues were 1.6 per cent lower compared with the corresponding period of 1998, in line with a targeted decrease of 1.5 per cent for the full year. On a cash basis, they rose by 1.5 per cent, against a budgeted increase of 4.2 per cent for the year as a whole.

11. Up to October 1999 (on a cash basis) tax revenues from the VAT were 15.7 per cent higher than in the same period a year earlier.

12. In 1996, gross domestic investment in R&D amounted to 0.9 per cent of GDP, against 1.8 per cent on average in the EU and 2.2 per cent in the OECD area (OECD, STI database).

13. However, this will not affect the deficit on a national accounts basis as it corresponds to a below-the-line change in assets.

14. A structural inflation differential reflects faster productivity and wage growth in the traded goods sector owing to catch-up with the productivity level of higher-income economies. To keep up with more rapidly rising labour costs, prices in the non-traded goods sector (mostly services and construction), where productivity growth is slower, need to rise faster than in the traded goods sector. The increase in the relative price of non-traded goods prevents profitability from falling in that sector and is also reflected in higher overall consumer price inflation (the Balassa-Samuelson hypothesis). Lower-income euro-area countries can thus be expected to experience higher-than-average CPI inflation, mirrored by more rapidly increasing prices in services, owing to catching up of productivity in industry and other traded goods sectors.

15. According to the Regional Development Plans under elaboration, investment in less developed areas (Objective I) is projected to increase by 45 per cent in 2000-06 compared to 1994-99. Nevertheless, support from the EU structural and cohesion funds (which covered on average 40 per cent of infrastructure investment in 1993-99) will help fund infrastructure investment under the new Community Support Programme.

16. Should an indirect tax hike reduce the incentives for wage moderation from a lower tax wedge on labour income, the expected employment gains would be much weaker.

17. Estimates are drawn from OECD (1999h), Chapter IV: "The size and role of automatic fiscal stabilizers".

18. Territorial governments comprise both regional governments (autonomous communities) and local administrations. The budget deficit of the consolidated territorial governments mainly reflects the financial deficit of regional governments, as the financial accounts of local administrations are practically balanced. The data referred to thereafter are from Bank of Spain, "Financial accounts of the Spanish economy 1989-1998 ".

19. Local public enterprises have been expanding rapidly, with their number increasing by 45 per cent from 1990 to 1996. In the mid 1990s, these enterprises were receiving 20 per cent of total operating and capital transfers paid to public enterprises. See OECD (1998c), Chapter IV.

20. The projections were finalised in November 1999, based on data for the State budget available up to September 1999, and are identical to those released in the OECD *Economic Outlook* No. 66. Recent data since the projections in Table 8 were finalised point specifically to stronger than initially expected growth in tax revenues, and may herald a stronger than projected decline in the budget deficit.

21. The 2000 budget reduces employers' contribution rate for the unemployment insurance by 0.2 percentage points but eligibility conditions for reduced social security contributions on new permanent contracts have been tightened. In particular, the

conversion of a temporary contract into a permanent contract no longer gives right to reduced social security contributions.

22. In 1998, the unemployment rate of men aged 25 to 54 was 11.6 per cent, against 18.8 per cent for the average rate of unemployment. The corresponding unemployment rates for young workers, 16 to 19 year olds, and 20 to 24 year olds, were 44.8 and 32.8 per cent, respectively. The unemployment rate for women aged 25 to 54 was 24.1 per cent.

23. In a ranking of participation rates in job-related training programmes using an index that combines different sources of data, Spain ranked 19 among 24 OECD countries (OECD, 1999*f*).

24. Jimeno and Toharia (1992) show that an increase of 1 per cent in the temporary contract share is associated with a fall of 0.1 per cent in sectoral productivity growth. However, Hernando and Vallés (1992) do not confirm such an effect on total factor productivity growth.

25. Average job tenure has decreased from 11.5 years in 1985 to 9.1 in 1995. Similarly, the percentage of workers with tenure below one year has increased from 15.2 per cent to 24.8 per cent in the same period.

26. Average employee tenure for those under 25 is one year, against 8.9 years for the average employee (OECD, 1999*g*).

27. Though different wages for the same type of work are illegal, it seems that employers have been relatively free in classifying workers in different occupations, thus effectively paying less to fixed-term employees (Bentolila and Dolado, 1994).

28. Severance payments amount to 20 days of salary per year of work in the case of "justified" dismissals, against 45 days for unjustified dismissals.

29. As is the case for all indices elaborated with scores assigned to regulations, they can have weaknesses. For example, the index for the strictness of permanent employment is higher in Portugal than in Spain, whereas some evidence suggests that this is not the case (Bover *et al.*, 1998). The different interpretation lies in considering the attitude of tribunals in favour of workers when declaring most dismissals as unjustified.

30. Under the previous legislation, part-time contracts received pension rights which were less than proportional to the number of hours worked with respect to full-time workers.

31. Complementary hours are a new concept of working time defined for these contracts, which is similar to overtime but paid at the same rate as normal hours. Complementary hours can only be used for permanent contracts, and need the agreement of the worker. They cannot be more than 15 per cent of normal hours (or 30 per cent if allowed by a collective agreement). They have to be distributed proportionally by quarters, and only 30 per cent of hours agreed and not worked in a given quarter can be transferred to the following quarter.

32. In this respect, the influence of unemployment benefits on unemployment duration is well documented for Spain (Alba and Freeman, 1990; Cebrián *et al.*, 1995; Bover *et al.*, 1996). For a skeptical view, see Toharia (1997).

33. This does not include direct subsidies to employment or reductions in social security contributions for different types of contracts.

34. Civil servants in these regions account for less than 15 per cent of total regional public employment.

35. According to the labour force survey, in 1998, only 26 per cent among the unemployed would have accepted a job involving a change in residence, while 63.7 per cent would have accepted a job at a level lower than expected. These numbers have been declining since 1996, as labour market slack has been easing.

36. Discrepancies of regional wages to the national average (Wagegap) have been adjusted for differences in per capita regional GDP to the national average (Gdpgap) by estimating the following least squares regression:

    Wagegap = –0.075 + 0.395 . Gdpgap ; R2 = 0.34; t-statistics in brackets.
              (2.8)   (2.9)

    Adjusted wage differentials (Wagegap*) shown in Figure 12, panel B are the residuals of this regression. They show differences in wages across regions not accounted for by differences in per capita GDP. Regional per capita GDP is computed at factor cost from 1995 data. The 1998 labour market survey was used to compute wage differentials.

37. Aid to industry is mainly channelled through regular grants (29 per cent), tax concessions (22 per cent) and other mixed schemes (40 per cent) (OECD, 1998b). This is broadly in line with the average pattern found in OECD countries.

38. This is, however, by no means peculiar to Spain. In 1995-97, State aid to the transport sector in the European Union accounted for 35 per cent of overall national aid and was almost equivalent to the amount of aid granted to the manufacturing industry.

39. Owing to reduced debt servicing, RENFE's results have recently improved and allowed to slash State transfers by 15 per cent in 1998.

40. *Ministerio de Agricultura, Pesca y Alimentación* (1998). Additional aid *via* price support and export subsidies can not be evaluated on a country-by-country basis in the EU.

41. Main components of budgetary transfers include direct payments based on output, on area planted/animal numbers, on historical entitlements, on input use, on input constraints, and on overall farming income. Budgetary support has been on an upward trend in OECD countries. In the European Union, measured as a share of producer support estimate, it has increased from 16 per cent in 1986-88 to 48 per cent in 1996-98. In contrast, the share of market price support has been reduced from 84 per cent in 1986-88 to 52 per cent in 1996-98 (OECD, 1999a).

42. This requirement is similar to requirements imposed elsewhere in the EU. The decision on the merger should be made public within three months.

43. The public participation in Red Eléctrica has already been reduced from 60 to 25 per cent.

44. Developing interconnections with France raises environmental concerns and electricity prices in Portugal and Morocco are higher than domestic prices.

45. There is, for instance, a tax on electricity consumption to subsidise the restructuring of the domestic coal industry, which accounts for 28 per cent of fuel in electricity generation. The European Commission is currently examining the size of, and the guarantees attached to, the payments to utilities for the so-called costs of the transition to competition (the guarantees consist of allowing utilities to issue highly rated securities against the expected cash-flow).

46. In October 1999, the government also cut VAT rates on gas canisters from 16 to 7 per cent and eliminated the hydrocarbon tax.

47. Approximately 90 per cent of the petrol stations operate on concession agreements with the wholesale/refining companies. These contracts have fixed margins and are of long duration.

48. The maximum discount allowed on school books has recently been raised from 5 to 12 per cent.

49. Those mergers have reduced the number of big players in the Spanish banking system from five in 1998 to three: BSCH, BBVA and *Banco Popular*. BBV was created in 1988, after *Banco de Bilbao* merged with *Banco de Vizcaya*. BCH was formed in 1992 after the merger of *Banco Central* and *Banco Hispano*. Banco de Santander acquired *Banesto* in 1994. *Argentaria*, previously under public ownership, was privatised in 1998.

50. Other specific measures include: *a*) investments in the region have to be in long-term strategic positions; *b*) Spanish banks are required to retain full control over the management of the acquired banks; *c*) strict criteria are applied for risk provisioning and goodwill has been mostly redeemed; *d*) banks are required to fully hedge exchange rate risk.

51. The most active banks in Latin America have been Banco Bilbao Vizcaya and Banco Santander Central Hispano. Examples of major shareholdings of those two banks in Latin America are provided in Table A2. In spite of financial instability and rising interest rates in Latin America, Spanish banks have shown robust results up to now. For instance, according to 1998 results, Santander's trading income has dropped – partly on account of financial instability in Latin America – but this has been comfortably offset by an increase in earnings from fees and commissions, thanks to the strength of the group's operations in retail banking.

52. There are various other proxies for bank efficiency (Berger, 1993) – for instance, operating cost/income ratio; interest rate margin; labour cost share; and various measures of branch intensity. In 1997, the widely watched cost/income ratio (operating expenses over gross operating margin) was 59 and 63 per cent respectively for savings banks and commercial banks – broadly comparable to that of other OECD European countries, for instance Germany (64 per cent), but somewhat lower than that in France or the Netherlands (69 per cent). Nevertheless, this ratio should be interpreted carefully. In the presence of strong competition, squeezing the operating margins of banks, this ratio should be rather high, indicating high efficiency. On the other hand, with weak competition, if banks set margins for instance as a mark up on costs, a high cost/income ratio could reflect poor efficiency resulting from high operating expenses. In the increasingly competitive banking sectors in Europe, the first view seems more likely. This would point to lower efficiency of Spanish savings banks compared with commercial banks, while the Spanish banking system as a whole would post a lower level of efficiency than in some other best-practice European countries. At a more technical level, bank efficiency can be assessed using a stochastic cost frontier or a stochastic production frontier approach. According to a recent comparative study along these lines (Bikker, 1999), bearing on a sample of 3 000 European banks, estimated efficiency of Spanish banks turns out to be significantly lower than in other European countries.

53. The increase in the number of branches partly reflects the expansion of savings banks out of their region of origin, in search for bigger market share and looking for better-diversified risks. The geographical expansion of savings banks was restricted until 1989. On the other hand, commercial banks have been reducing their branches.

54. Responding to the increasingly complex financial environment, the Spanish banking supervisory authorities pay special attention to the largest credit institutions. Close control over their activities is carried out in two ways: *a*) on-site inspections and regular meetings with the heads of the different business areas; *b*) assessment of internal risk management processes with minimum standards that all institutions need to fulfil.

55. Around 25 per cent of savings banks' assets consist of mortgage credits, against 10 per cent for commercial banks. Moreover, though the operations of both kinds of institutions have been converging, savings banks invest relatively more than commercial banks in central government securities – especially in long-term bonds. Despite the regional origin of savings banks, their lending to regional governments does not surpass that of commercial banks. There are nearly 50 savings banks in Spain, though the 12 largest account for about 70 per cent of the sector's total assets. The two largest, La Caixa and Caja Madrid, account for 35 per cent of total assets.

56. *Costes y tarifas de los mercados españoles de valores* (1999).

57. At the end of 1997, assets of investment funds amounted to 35 per cent of GDP, as against 31.3 per cent in the euro area (weighted average). The potential erosion of profitability of the banking system has been muted, however, since funds that account for a large part of the assets of collective investment institutions are managed by institutions belonging to commercial and savings banks groups.

58. The most prominent measures include a widening of the pension base to the last 15 years of contributions, a gradual rise of the contribution ceilings to the highest one, and an agreement to finance non-contributory pensions by general taxation (see the previous survey).

59. Large immigration flows could contribute to mitigate somewhat the rise in the dependency ratio. Official demographic projections presented in Figure 17 incorporate assumptions of a rapidly rising net migration flow (from 44 thousand in 1998 to 289 thousand in 2050) and a recovery in the birth rate from 1.2 in 1998 to 1.7 in 2020.

60. Chapter III reports simulations on this.

61. The implicit tax rate on continuing work displays the foregone pensions – resulting from postponing retirement from 55 to 64 – as a share of additional earnings from work and accrual of higher pension entitlements due to the increase in the years of contributions. All else equal, the higher the working income replacement rate and the lower the accrual rate of pension rights in the late working years, the higher the implicit tax rate on continuing work. For the methodology of these calculations, see Blondal and Scarpetta (1997). In addition, in many countries, non-employment benefits received by old-age workers (mainly unemployment and disability benefits) have been turned into *de facto* early retirement benefits. Withdrawal of these benefits, if added to foregone pension payments due to postponed retirement, may significantly raise the disincentives for continuing work.

62. Incentives for early retirement appear much stronger when taking into account means-tested non-employment benefits. Among OECD countries, Spain turned out to have one of the highest implicit tax rates on continuing work in 1995, involving a pre-tax gain of only half the additional gross income from postponing retirement.

63. The annual cost amounted to an estimated ESP 100 billion in 1998 and 1999.

64. Significant progress has been achieved in the fight against fraud over the past years, in particular for the temporary disability scheme and the minimum old-age pension (*complemento de mínimos*).

65. These simulations have been performed, and provided, by the research department of the Banco Bilbao Vizcaya.

66. Health responsibilities have been devolved to seven regions: Andalucía, Canarias, Cataluña, Galicia, Navarra, País Vasco, and Valencia.

67. Contributions to private health insurance paid by an employee's company are considered as payments in kind and are tax exempt up to ESP 60 000 for individuals and up to ESP 200 000 when the insurance covers the spouse and children.

68. A change in the legal status of existing public hospitals is conditional on the personnel's agreement.

69. The regional government of Valencia envisages implementing such a model.

70. Expenditures on pharmaceuticals amounted to ESP 950 billion in 1998, 1.1 per cent of GDP.

71. Wholesalers' and pharmacists' margins were already cut in 1993, 1997 and 1999. In July 1999, the government approved an average 6 per cent cut in pharmaceutical prices.

72. Non-pensioners pay 40 per cent of the cost of pharmaceuticals in primary care. Overall, however, the average co-payment stands at around 8 per cent since pensioners account for 75 per cent of public expenditure on pharmaceuticals.

73. The large and continuous drop in public enterprise jobs reflects the vast privatisation programme carried out throughout the decade.

74. The future trends of the social security system are examined in OECD (1996).

75. As proxy indicators of infrastructure endowment in Spain, paved roads and railroad tracks per square km amounted to 0.48 and 0.04 kms respectively at the beginning of the 1990s. The corresponding indicators for France, Germany and Italy were: for paved roads, 1.35, 1.42, 1.03, and for railroad tracks, 0.06, 0.12, 0.09. Calculations are based on World Bank (1994).

76. In 1995, social security expenditure (excluding unemployment benefits) were funded up to two-thirds by employers' and employees' social security contributions and for the rest by government transfers (that is, by general taxation). As it is unlikely that wage earners perceive social security payments as part of their income (which could be the case if contributions were set on an actuarially fair insurance basis), the wedge is likely to be adverse for employment. This could be so either in terms of reduced labour supply if net wages are reduced, or in terms of labour demand if they are not. This is likely to be the case in pay-as-you-go systems where increases in contributions are often not linked to a marginal improvement in expected benefits.

77. Before June 1996, capital gains were not taxed once the legally established period, generally 10 years, had elapsed. From June 1996, a 20 per cent flat rate was established on capital gains obtained on assets held more than two years.

78. These data on expenditures exclude interest payments. In 1998, regional and local governments accounted for 74 per cent of general government investment (Ministerio de Administraciones Públicas, 1999).

79. The budgeted increase in ceded taxes was tied to the growth of a basket of taxes (including the personal and corporate income taxes as well as the VAT).

80. Competences transferred include: education, social services, active labour market policies, some infrastructure investment, and health. In January 2000, the transfer of

health responsibilities will not have been completed in 9 regions, while the process of decentralisation of primary and secondary education will be still pending in two regions.

81. Ministerio de Economía y Hacienda (1998*f*).

82. See Instituto de Estudios Fiscales (1998). According to a survey realised by the *Centro de Investigaciones Sociológicas* in 1998, 92 per cent of people interviewed considered that personal income tax fraud was significant.

83. See Ministerio de Economía y Hacienda (1998*g*).

84. Sanctions vary between 35 and 150 per cent of the tax due. The period required to resolve a conflict can last up to 7 years.

85. See Instituto de Estudios Fiscales (1998), p. 158, and Instituto de Estudios Fiscales (1994).

86. Presumptions of a large overstatement of expenditures and misrepresentation of the characteristics of the tax unit concern the report of expenses related to the acquisition of a secondary residence as those for a main residence, overstating health expenditures, and considering a person as disabled. See Ministerio de Economía y Hacienda (1998*b*); Ministerio de Economía y Hacienda (1998*c*); Ministerio de Economía y Hacienda (1998*d*). See also Confederación Sindical de Comisiones Obreras (1998).

87. See Martín and García Lopez (1999). According to the *Memoria Económica del Anteproyecto de Ley de Reforma del* IRPF, the average taxpayer devoted one and a half hours to file tax returns and spent ESP 8 000 (opportunity costs and fees paid to tax advisers).

88. Delays to process tax returns were cut for the personal income tax: from 110 days in 1995 to 66 in 1998, and a further reduction to 55 days is envisaged for 1999. Assistance to taxpayers has been developed, in particular through tax filing assistance by telephone. The *Programa de ayuda a la declaración de la renta* concerned 11 million tax declarations (15 million declarations were sent to the tax administration in 1998). From 1999, taxpayers have been able to file tax returns through the Internet.

89. Maximum 12 months for tax inspections, 4 years for tax prescriptions and 6 months for tax refunds (after this 6-month period, interest is paid by the administration).

90. From 1999, a taxpayer moving to a tax haven will continue to pay taxes in Spain during four years. To limit coupon-washing operations (which consist of selling and repurchasing domestic shares on international stock markets to reduce residents' tax burden), tax credits for dividends will no longer be granted for shares bought less than two months before, and sold less than two months after, the dividend disbursement.

91. The Spanish social security system includes a general regime and many special regimes applying to various professional categories. Following measures introduced in 1998, these special regimes are to be progressively harmonised with the general regime. The general regime and each category have a minimum (which is independent of the wage) and a maximum monthly basis for determining the amount of contributions.

92. This is not shown in Figure 23 as the income corresponding to the minimum wage is less than half an average production worker's income.

93. Low-skilled labour tends to be a good substitute for other production inputs (*e.g.* capital, energy). As a result, the high elasticity of substitution of low-skilled

labour with these factors is reflected in a high own-wage elasticity. For discussion of available evidence see OECD (1995).

94. This follows as an application of the "Ramsey rule" for optimal taxation. The excess burden of a tax is an additional cost to society, over the amount of tax collected by the state. It arises when a price-distorting tax prevents markets from attaining efficient output levels, owing to the price of taxed goods being different from marginal private benefits and costs. Taxes with minimum excess burden are those levied on goods and services that are in inelastic supply, demand, or both – as in those cases market responses to distortions are subdued.

95. In some cases, after-tax labour earnings were reportedly even lower than out-of-work transfer income. This had been reflected in *effective* marginal tax rates of close to 100 per cent at low-income levels that might have been at the origin of unemployment traps. See OECD (1994a).

96. Unemployment benefits became taxed after the 1994 labour market reform with the exception of those received as lump-sum payments, to be used for the creation of a new business; to participate in a worker-owned limited company (*Sociedad Laboral*) or in a cooperative company; and for handicapped people who want to set up a business. In these four cases, unemployment benefits are tax-exempt up to ESP 1 000 000 (this treshold was increased in May 1999 from ESP 500 000).

97. Mandatory compensation received as severance pay or for termination of employment is tax exempt up to the maximum legal amount as defined in the Labour Code.

98. Personal income tax relief is estimated at 11.7 per cent of tax liabilities of the taxpayer with labour earnings at the APW level – that is, around 2 000 000 pesetas. The estimated impact of the personal income tax reform on individual tax liabilities are provided in "Memoria Económica del Anteproyecto de Ley de Reforma del IRPF", p. 31.

99. See also OECD (1995). An analysis of these points can also be found in Pissarides (1998).

100. Tax expenditure does not include the low taxation of imputed rents on owner-occupied housing.

101. Before 1999, interest expenses were deductible from the tax base – to which marginal rates apply – though with a ESP 800 000 ceiling for an individual (ESP 1 000 000 for a joint declaration), and principal repayments entitled to a reduction in the total tax due.

102. Before the 1998 personal income tax reform, an imputed income – calculated at 2 per cent of the catastral value of the taxpayer's home if the catastral value had not been reestimated before 1994, and at 1.1 per cent otherwise – was included in the taxable income. However, imputed rent was unrealistically low, largely because the housing market value was much higher than recorded in the land register (about 50 per cent).

103. The 1998 personal income tax reform abolished: a) the ESP 29 000 tax exemption on capital income; b) the exemption of capital gains when the sale value was inferior to ESP 500 000; c) the zero-tax rate applied on the first ESP 200 000 capital gains; and d) the revaluation coefficient on equities (used to correct capital gains for past inflation). The new personal income tax only maintains the revaluation coefficient for real estate assets.

104. Investment in pension funds is deductible from taxable income up to ESP 1.1 million or 20 per cent of labour income (the lower amount is binding). For people older than

52, the deduction can be higher and reach ESP 2.2 million for 65 year old persons. Since the 1998 personal income tax reform, contributions to life insurance contracts do no longer give rise to a tax credit. For pension funds and insurance schemes, tax is deferred until the taxpayer is eligible to withdraw money from the fund. Annuities are fully taxed with other labour income. For lump-sum payments, the taxable income is defined as the difference between the premium and the payment. Tax rates on these capital gains vary, as for other financial income, according to the holding period (Table 18).

105. A high-income individual will pay 48 per cent on T-bill income. If the person holds the same T-bill through collective investment institutions, he will only pay a 20 per cent tax rate.

106. Households are not subject to tax on capital gains if financial assets have been held for more than one year in Austria and in Germany.

107. Buijink, Janssen and Schols (1999).

108. These estimates are drawn from the consolidated financial statement data of a panel of 2 118 European Union, mainly listed, manufacturing companies – excluding therefore important sectors such as insurance and financial services. As data are drawn from income statements published by the firms in the sample, cross-country differences in effective tax rates may also partly reflect differences in accounting practices.

109. The corporate income tax includes also provisions for partial or total (under the "Affiliation privilege") relief of double taxation of domestic inter-company dividend distributions.

110. In the 2000 State Budget, tax expenditures are projected to amount to 20.9 per cent of gross corporate income tax liabilities.

111. Tax wedges are computed using the King-Fullerton method – see Gordon, K. and H. Tchilinguirian (1998). They assess the pre-tax rate of return an investment must earn to be worthwhile from the standpoint of the company's shareholders – which may, as an alternative, invest in a risk-free bank deposit. Since the ultimate decision-maker is the individual shareholder, his personal income tax liabilities (against interest, dividends, and capital gains earned on firms' investments) are added to the corporate income tax to assess the overall pre-tax profitability of investments. To focus on cross-country differences related only to the tax system – abstracting thus from interactions induced by differences in inflation – the estimates reported in Table 19 were computed assuming the same inflation rate across countries of 2 per cent.

112. In 1997, the government levied a 3 per cent tax on the capital gains arising from the (voluntary) revaluation of firms' assets. Despite this, most companies preferred to revalue their assets to reduce their future tax burden and improve their access to capital markets through improved capitalisation.

113. As an exception to the overall tax neutrality towards physical investment comes, however, the special regime applying to mining companies, which are entitled to a reduction in taxable profits of up to 30 per cent.

114. This calculation is based on statutory corporate tax rates and on the top-income earner tax rate. Because of various corporate tax incentives, which vary across countries, effective corporate tax rates are much lower than statutory rates. Their cross-country comparability is subject to caveats. For instance, in Spain the effective

corporate tax rate amounted to 26 per cent in 1996, compared with a 35 per cent statutory rate.

115. A tax credit of 20 per cent of R&D expenses is available, which can rise up to 40 per cent for incremental expenses if their overall level is above that in the preceding two years on average. In addition, R&D investment (except buildings) may be freely depreciated over time. The government has further enhanced tax preferences to R&D investment within the 2000 budget law. Tax relief for R&D investment will be provided up to 50 per cent of tax liabilities – against 35 per cent for other types of investment tax credits. Additional public support in the form of investment subsidies and public credits is being planned with the aim of raising R&D expenditures to 1.2 per cent of GDP by 2003.

116. For a review of issues concerning training and a synthesis of empirical evidence see OECD (1991a).

117. Before the 1998 reform, deductions from the taxable income included: a lump sum of 5 per cent of wage earnings which could be deducted from the taxable income up to a maximum of ESP 250 000; mortgage interest payments related to the purchase of a main residence; severance payments up to the statutory maximum amount; contributions to pension schemes. Tax credits included: 15 per cent of health expenses; 15 per cent of the costs incurred in the year for the purchase or restoration of the taxpayer's primary residence; 10 per cent of the premiums for certain life insurance policies.

118. See Ministerio de Economía y Hacienda, Dirección General de Tributos (1998h).

119. Before the 1998 PIT reform, employees could deduct 5 per cent of their wage earnings from their taxable income. From 1999, tax allowances are declining with the level of gross earnings: set at ESP 500 000 for income below ESP 1 350 000, they drop to ESP 375 000 for incomes above ESP 2 000 000.

120. However, contributions to health insurance paid by employers are considered as payments in kind for employees and have been made tax-exempt up to ESP 60 000 for individuals and up to ESP 200 000 when the insurance covers the spouse and children.

121. Would a dynamic perspective be adopted, the impact of social security contributions on income redistribution would be less negative. The perspective adopted here is how taxes and transfers redistribute income among persons at any given point in time. Another aspect of the tax and transfer system is how it redistributes income over the life-cycle of the individual. For this analysis, breaking down transfers into two components would be necessary – those pertaining to redistribution over the life cycle, and those to inter-personal redistribution. Social security contributions associated with future income (pension) flows largely pertain to the first category.

122. Employees whose total compensation exceeds the maximum contribution base, or does not reach the minimum base for their category, pay social security contributions according to the maximum or the minimum payment, respectively. In 1999, the minimum social security contribution applied up to a ESP 80 820 monthly income.

123. Goods and services which are taxed at the super-reduced or reduced rates include: books, food, hotels, restaurants, drugs and medical services, water, private house acquisition (OECD, 1999d).

124. See OECD (1999e), for an estimation of the costs of reduced VAT rates and its distribution along the income scale.

125. The so-called "common regime" covers two groups of regions: those (called the Article 151 regions) which have taken more extensive spending powers – including health and education – and the others (Article 143 regions). The "fast-track" group of regions (Article 151) includes: Andalucía, Canarias, Cataluña, Galicia, Valencia. The others (Article 143) are: Aragón, Asturias, Baleares, Cantabria, Castilla La Mancha, Castilla y León, Extremadura, La Rioja, Madrid, Murcia.

126. The agreement stipulated that if a region's personal income tax revenues grew less than the national income, the central government would compensate through transfers up to 90 per cent of the rate of growth of the State personal income tax collection. For more details, see OECD (1998c), and Ezquiaga and García (1997).

127. Before 1997, the law stated that the share of the State's revenues transferred to regional governments would grow as the State's tax revenues, but in any case could not grow faster than GDP.

128. Past developments provide an indication of the likely frequency and magnitude of the transfers associated with the guarantee scheme: in 1995 and 1996, 8 and 12, respectively, out of the 15 common regime regions have had their personal income tax revenues growing less than the national GDP, and would thus have been entitled to compensating transfers had the guarantee scheme been in place. According to OECD Secretariat estimates for the period 1994-96, the cost of the personal income tax guarantees for the State would have amounted to around ESP 90 billion had the system been in place, with 50 billion in 1996 alone.

129. In 1997, personal income tax receipts grew less than the nominal GDP in all regions but the Canary Islands. State transfers required to compensate for this loss amount to ESP 33 billion. Furthermore, in the previous financing model the amount each region would receive from the so-called "share of the State revenues" could not grow faster than the nominal GDP. By removing this upward limit, the State had to transfer an additional ESP 60 billion (State revenues grew by 11.3 per cent in 1997, compared with a 5.46 per cent growth in nominal GDP). Because three regions (Andalucía, Castilla la Mancha and Extremadura) are not entitled to compensating transfers since they have refused this model, the total cost for the State budget stands below the estimated ESP 90 billion.

130. According to the analysis carried out by Carrasco et al. (1998), State transfers to the regions which will be required to compensate for the fall in the 15 per cent share of personal income tax revenues devolved to them, as a consequence of the 1998 reform, would amount to ESP 142 billion (close to 0.2 per cent of 1999 GDP).

131. See Ministerio de Economía y Hacienda (1998i). Taxes on land and real estate raised by local authorities include: the tax on real estate (IBI), the tax on the increase in the value of urban land, and the tax on construction and installations. The other main tax revenue stems from the tax on mechanically powered vehicles and the tax on economic activities.

132. The new State Land Regime and Valuation Law aimed at: ensuring a greater supply of developable land by changing the philosophy of the law on land uses (all land is now considered to be developable unless specifically ruled otherwise); speeding up planning processes; and reducing land charges (by bringing down from 15 to 10 the percentage of land, destined for lucrative use, owners must cede to local authorities).

133. One explanation, according to Castillo López (1999), is that the expected cost of sanctions is lower than wastewater charges or treatment costs.

134.   Water is highly subsidised in Spain: 80 to 90 per cent of the associated costs are financed through the State budget. See Castillo López J.M. (1999).

135. CO_2 emissions accounted for 71 per cent of Spain's total greenhouse gas emissions in 1990. Data on other greenhouse gas emissions are not available for more recent years.

136.   The main exception is the large differential in excise taxes between unleaded and leaded gasoline. On the other hand, there is no differentiation in heavy fuel oil taxation according to the sulphur content. There is an electricity tax, but it is not differentiated by carbon content. However, tax incentives are granted, through the corporate income tax system, to co-generation activities.

137.   In 1996, the effective VAT rate (VAT revenue as a share of consumption) in Spain was 4.3 percentage points below the (simple) average of European Union countries (according to OECD revenue statistics). The share of consumption in GDP is at present slightly over 60 per cent.

138.   See also OECD (1995). A formal analysis of these points can also be found in Pissarides (1998).

139.   In some EU countries, losses may be carried forward indefinitely to be set off against future profits (e.g. Germany, the United Kingdom and the Netherlands). Provisions for carrying backward losses also exist in Germany (one year), the United Kingdom (one year) and the Netherlands (three years).

140.   Examples of differences in the fiscal cost of inheritance transfers, according to compliance with existing regulations and tax exemptions, are given in De Aguiar (1998).

Glossary of acronyms

ALMP	Active Labour Market Policies
APW	Average Production Worker
BBV	Banco Bilbao Vizcaya
BCH	Banco Central Hispano
BSCH	Banco Santander Central Hispano
CAP	Common Agricultural Policy
CIT	Corporate Income Tax
CNMV	Comisión Nacional del Mercado de Valores (Stock Market Regulator)
CNSE	Comisión Nacional del Sistema Eléctrico (Regulatory body for electricity)
CPFF	Consejo de Política Fiscal y Financiera (Council for coordination of regional fiscal policies)
CPI	Consumer Price Index
EPA	Encuesta de Población Activa (Labour force survey)
EPL	Employment Protection Legislation
EU	European Union
FDI	Foreign direct investment
FEGA	Fondo Español de Garantía Agraria
FEOGA	Fondo Europeo de Orientación y Garantía Agrícola
GDP	Gross Domestic Product
GIF	Gestor de Infraestructuras Ferroviarias (Public entity responsible for several new railway works)
HICP	Harmonized index of consumer prices
INE	Instituto Nacional de Estadística
IPO	Initial Public Offering
IRPF	Impuesto sobre la renta de las personas físicas
METRs	Marginal Effective Tax Rates
ONIF	Oficina Nacional de Investigación del Fraude
PIE	Participación en los Ingresos del Estado (Share of the State tax revenues assigned to the regions)
R&D	Research and Development
RENFE	National Railway Company
RTVE	National Radio and Television Company
SEPI	Sociedad Estatal de Participaciones Industriales (Public holding controlling industrial public enterprises)
SGP	Stability and Growth Pact
SMEs	Small and Medium Enterprises
VAT	Value Added Tax

Bibliography

Alba, A. and R. Freeman (1990),
"Job finding and wages when long run unemployment is really long: the case of Spain",
NBER Working Paper No. 3409.

Basque Government (1998),
"Economic Agreement", Vitoria.

Bentolila, S. and J. J. Dolado (1994),
"Labour flexibility and wages: lessons from Spain", *Economic Policy*, No. 18, April.

Berger, A.N. (1993),
"The efficiency of financial institutions: A review and preview of research past, present
and future", *Journal of Banking and Finance*, Vol. 17, No. 2-3.

Besley, T. and P. Seabright (1999),
"The effects and Policy implications of state aids to industry: an economic analysis",
Economic Policy, No. 28, April.

Bikker, J. A. (1999),
"Efficiency in the European banking industry: an exploratory analysis to rank countries", De Nederlandsce Bank, Staff Reports, No. 42, October.

Blöndal, S. and S. Scarpetta (1997),
"Early retirement in OECD countries: The role of social security systems", OECD
Economic Studies, No. 29, 1997. *http://www.oecd.org/eco/stud/stud29.htm#retire.*

Bover, O., M. Arellano and S. Bentolila (1996),
"Unemployment duration, benefit duration and the business cycle", Bank of Spain,
Economic Studies, No. 57.

Bover, O., P. García-Perea and P. Portugal (1998),
"A Comparative Study of the Portuguese and Spanish Labour Markets", Bank of Spain,
Working Paper No. 9807.

Buijink, W., B. Janssen and Y. Schols (1999),
"Corporate Effective Tax Rates in the European Union", Maastricht Accounting and
Auditing Research and Education Centre, April.

Carrasco, C., J. Onrubia and R. Paredes (1998),
"Análisis de los efectos recaudatorios y redistributivos de la reforma del IRPF por
Comunidades Autónomas", Instituto de Estudios Fiscales, Working Paper No. 19/98.

Cassela, A. (1999),
"Tradable deficit permits: efficient implementation of the Stability Pact in the EMU",
NBER, Working Paper No. 7278.

Castillo López, J.M. (1999),
"Los tributos ecológicos y la calidad de los recursos hídricos continentales", Boletín Económico del ICE, No. 2616.

Cebrián, I., C. García, J. Muro, L. Toharia and E. Villagómez (1995),
"Prestaciones por desempleo duración del paro y desempleo recurrente", in J.J. Dolado and J.F. Jimeno (eds.), Estudios sobre el mercado de trabajo en España, FEDEA, Madrid.

Coase, R. (1960),
"The problem of social cost", Journal of Law and Economics, No. 3.

Confederación Sindical de Comisiones Obreras (1998),
Situación de la economía española y presupuestos del Estado 1999, Cuadernos de Información Sindical.

Dalsgaard, T. and A. De Serres, (1999),
"Estimating prudent budgetary margins for 11 EU countries: A simulated SVAR model approach", OECD Economics Department Working Papers, No. 216.

De Aguiar, E. (1998),
"Beneficios fiscales en la empresa familiar: patrimonio y sucesiones", La Caixa, pp. 76-78, Barcelona.

Dolado, J., J. M. González-Páramo and J. Viñals (1997),
"A cost-benefit analysis of going from low inflation to price stability in Spain", Bank of Spain, Working Paper No. 9728.

Draper, M. (1993),
"Indiciación salarial y empleo", Moneda y Crédito, No. 197.

Echebarría, K. (1998),
"User charging at the Barcelona fire Department", Occasional Papers, No. 22, Public Management, Paris. http://www.oecd.org/puma/mgmtres/cards.htm#ucgs98.

Elmeskov, J. Martin and S. Scarpetta (1999),
"Key lessons for labour market reforms: Evidence from OECD countries' experience", Swedish Economic Policy Review, forthcoming.

Ezquiaga, I. and F. García (1997),
"Una evaluacion del sistema de Financiación autonómica para el quinquenio 1997-2001", Cuadernos de información económica, No. 120-121, March-April.

García-Serrano, C. and J.F. Jimeno (1998),
"Labour reallocation, job tenure, labour flows and labour market institutions: Evidence from Spain", Fedea, Working paper No. 98-07.

Gordon, K. and H. Tchilinguirian (1998),
"Marginal effective tax rates on physical, human and R&D capital", OECD Economics Department Working Papers, No. 199, Paris. http://www.olis.oecd.org/olis/1998doc.nsf.

Grupo de trabajo Bolsas-SCLV-MEFF-CNMV (1999),
Costes y tarifas de los mercados españoles de valores, mimeo.

Hernando, R. and J. Vallés (1993),
"Productividad, situación de mercado y situación financiera", Bank of Spain, Working Paper No. 9227.

Huguet, A. (1999),
"Testing Spanish labour market segmentation: an unknown-regime approach", Applied Economics, No. 31.

Instituto de Estudios Fiscales (1994),
   Informe sobre el fraude en España, p. 71, Madrid.

Instituto de Estudios Fiscales (1998),
   Informe para la reforma del impuesto sobre la renta de las personas físicas, p. 158, Madrid.

Jiménez-Martín, S. (1998),
   "Indexation and wage change settlement: evidence from Spanish manufacturing firms", *Oxford Bulletin of Economics and Statistics*, Vol. 60, No. 4.

Jimeno, J.F. and L. Toharia (1992),
   "Productivity and Wage Effects of Fixed-Term Employment: The case of Spain", FEDEA, Working Paper No. 9211, Madrid.

La Caixa (1999*b*),
   Monthly Report, May 1999.

Lambarri, C. and A. van Mourik (1998),
   "Tax harmonisation: the case of the economic Agreement between Spain and the Basque country", Fundación BBV, European Institute of Public Administration, Maastricht.

Martín F., A. and J. García Lopez (1999),
   "Creencias y actitudes de los contribuyentes", *Cuadernos de Información económica*, No. 146, May 1999.

Ministerio de Administraciones Públicas (1999),
   Informe Económico-Financiero de la Administraciones Territoriales en 1997, Madrid.

Ministerio de Agricultura, Pesca y Alimentación (1998),
   "La Agricultura, la Pesca y la Alimentación en 1998", Madrid.

Ministerio de Economía y Hacienda (1998*a*),
   "Recaudación y Estadísticas de la Reforma Tributaria (1987-97)", Madrid.

Ministerio de Economía y Hacienda (1998*b*),
   "Análisis estadístico de la deducción por inversión en la vivienda habitual (IRPF 1996)", Madrid.

Ministerio de Economía y Hacienda (1998*c*),
   "La deducciones familiares en el IRPF (1986-96)" Madrid.

Ministerio de Economía y Hacienda (1998*d*),
   "Deducciones por gastos de enfermedad en el IRPF (1985-96)", Madrid.

Ministerio de Economía y Hacienda (1998*e*),
   "Valoración del impuesto sobre la renta de las pensiones físicas 1996", Madrid.

Ministerio de Economía y Hacienda (1998*f*),
   "Los costes de gestión de la administración tributaria en 1996", Dirección General de Tributos, Madrid.

Ministerio de Economía y Hacienda, (1998*g*),
   "Balance de la ejecución del Plan bianual para la mejora del cumplimiento fiscal y la lucha contra el fraude tributario y aduanero aprobado por acuerdo del Consejo de Ministros de 5 julio de 1996", Dirección General de Tributos, Madrid.

Ministerio de Economía y Hacienda (1998*h*),
   "La estructura de la cuota líquida según fuentes de renta (ejercicio 1996)", Madrid.

Mishkin, F.S. (1999),
"Financial Consolidation: Dangers and opportunities", *Journal of Banking and Finance*, No. 23.

Moreno Seijas, J.M. (1998),
"La tasa y el precio público como instrumetos de financiación", Working Paper No. 7/98, Instituto de Estudios Fiscales.

OECD (1991*a*),
Employment Outlook, July, Paris.

OECD (1991*b*),
"Taxing Profits in a Global Economy: Domestic and International Issues", Paris.

OECD (1994*a*),
Economic Survey of Spain, Paris.

OECD (1994*b*),
"Taxation and small businesses", Paris.

OECD (1994*c*),
"Taxation and household saving", Paris.

OECD (1995),
The OECD Jobs Study: Taxation, Employment and Unemployment, Paris.

OECD (1996),
Economic Survey of Spain, Paris.

OECD (1998*a*),
Labour force Survey, Paris.

OECD (1998*b*),
Spotlight on Public Support to Industry, Paris.

OECD (1998*c*),
Economic Survey of Spain, Paris.

OECD (1998*d*),
Labour Force Statistics, Paris.

OECD (1998*e*),
"Harmful tax competition: An emerging global issue", Paris.

OECD (1999*a*),
Agricultural Policies in OECD Countries: Monitoring and Evaluation, Paris.

OECD (1999*b*),
"The role of competition policy in regulatory reform", *Regulatory Reform in Spain*, Chapter III, Paris.

OECD (1999*c*),
"Regulatory Reform in the Telecommunications industry: Spain", Working Party on Telecommunications and Information Services Policies, 19-20 April 1999, Paris.

OECD (1999*d*),
Consumption tax trends, Paris.

OECD (1999*e*),
Economic Survey of Mexico, Paris.

OECD (1999*f*),
Employment Outlook, Chapter 3, "Training of Adult Workers in OECD Countries: Measurement and Analysis", Paris

OECD (1999*g*),
The OECD Jobs Strategy: Assessing Performance and Policy, Paris.

OECD (1999*h*),
OECD Economic Outlook, December, No. 66, Paris.

Oswald, A. J. (1997),
"The missing piece of the Unemployment puzzle, an inaugural lecture", mimeo presented to an OECD informal workshop.

Petitbó J., A. E. Povedano Moreno (1998),
"La competencia en el mercado del suelo", Cuadernos Gallegos de Economía, No. 2.

Pissarides, C. (1998),
"The impact of employment tax cuts on unemployment and wages: The role of unemployment benefits and tax structure", European Economic Review, No. 42.

Roeger, W. and J. in't Veld (1997),
"Quest II A multi country business cycle and growth model", Economic Papers, No. 123, European Commission, DG II.

Roeger, W. and J. in't Veld (1998),
"The macroeconomic effects of tax reforms in the Quest model", mimeo, European Commission, DG II.

Ruiz Castillo J., E. Ley and M. Izquierdo (1999),
"La medición de la inflacion en España", La Caixa, Colección Estudios e Informes, No.°17.

Sáez, F. (1997),
"Políticas de mercado de trabajo en España y en Europa", Papeles de Economía Española, No. 72.

Serrano, G., J.F. Jimeno (1998),
"Labour reallocation, job tenure, labour flows and labour market institutions: Evidence from Spain", FEDEA, Working Paper No. 9807.

Serrano Leal, C. (1996),
"La reforma del impuesto sobre sociedades en España", Boletín Económico del ICE, No. 2523.

Toharia, L. (1997),
"El sistema español de protección por desempleo", Papeles de Economía Española, No. 72.

World Bank (1994),
"World Development Report: Infrastructure for Development", Washington D.C.

Annex I

SMEs and self-employed: special tax regimes

Among Spain's 3.7 million enterprises (in the mid-1990s) 75 per cent are one-person businesses and 22 per cent are micro-enterprises with less than 10 employees. The share of self-employed is much higher than elsewhere in the European Union (50 per cent), probably reflecting extensive subcontracting arrangements owing to strict employment protection legislation.

A special tax regime applies, first, to incorporated small businesses with turnover of less than ESP 250 million. They benefit from a reduced corporate tax rate of 30 per cent, up to the first ESP 15 million of taxable profits – additional profits being taxed at the normal 35 per cent rate.* Moreover, they may benefit from more liberal depreciation allowances for new tangible assets.

Unincorporated businesses, self-employed and other professionals are subject to the personal income tax, and may qualify for special simplified regimes. While SMEs with turnover of more than ESP 100 million are subject to a "direct estimation" system, involving fully-fledged accounting rules, SMEs below this threshold may choose between two simpler schemes. A "simplified direct estimation" system, based on less complex accounting rules, and a "forfaitaire" system (*"módulos"*) relying on objective assessment of taxable income.

The *"módulos"* system was introduced in 1992. The "simplified direct estimation system" came into effect in 1998. It replaced the "simplified flat rate system" (*"estimación objetiva por coeficientes"*) which was a mixture of a "forfaitaire" system and estimation based on accounting rules. In 1996, among 2 463 000 unincorporated businesses subject to those three regimes of the personal income tax, 75 per cent (half of which in agriculture) were taxed according to the "forfaitaire" system; 10 per cent according to the "simplified flat rate" system; and the remaining 15 per cent according to "direct estimation".

Both systems allow depreciation deductions for tangible assets according to simplified rules. Income assessment under the "forfaitaire" system relies on business activity indicators – for instance the number of employees, power consumption, workshop surface, etc. This scheme was initially introduced with the aim of containing tax avoidance and simplifying tax compliance for micro-enterprises and self-employed. It has evolved into a highly complex system of tax assessment, covering at present 84 sectors, with specific provisions for each of them.

---

* In 1996, 55 per cent of companies subject to corporate income tax reported profits below ESP 25 million, whereas 36 per cent had profits lower than ESP 10 million. Under the Basque Country and Navarra special tax regimes, a reduced rate of 30 per cent applies up to the first ESP 10 million of taxable income for qualifying SMEs. Above that amount, profits are taxed at the standard 32.5 per cent corporate tax rate.

Annex II

Shifting the tax mix: properties of model-based simulations

The results presented in the tax chapter (Table 23) refer to the long-run for the Quest II (European Commission) model (Roeger and in't Veld, 1997; 1998), when most macroeconomic adjustments following the tax changes have been completed, and to a four-year period for Interlink. Though the simulation period in the Quest model extends up to 30 years, a large part of the adjustments (ranging from 66 to 80 per cent depending on the tax) occurs within a 10-year period. The simulations assume that monetary policy responds to tax and spending cuts so as to keep inflation at the baseline. All tax changes are revenue neutral, being offset by an equal reduction in transfer payments or by an increase in other taxes. Compared with other taxes, cutting corporate income taxes appears to have the highest long-run impact on GDP (Table 23). This reflects the strong impact of a reduced corporate tax rate on companies' profitability and thereby on investment. The employment impact of a corporate tax cut is relatively weak, however, owing to factor substitution. In contrast, a cut in labour taxes has the strongest long-run impact on employ-ment, as it increases directly the demand for labour. The OECD Interlink model projects an increase in GDP similar to the Commission's Quest model and a slightly stronger response of employment. Reduced consumption taxes turn out to be the least powerful instrument to boost GDP growth and employment.

According to the simulations, output and employment effects of tax cuts might be muted in Spain by pervasive labour market rigidities, which are discussed in the main text. A main difference to other countries pertaining to the labour market in the Spanish version of the Quest model is a higher trade union bargaining strength – as measured by the indexation of real wages to productivity trends. On account of these rigidities, tax cuts translate more than elsewhere in the European Union into higher wages. That undermines competitiveness and dampens the rise in employment and output. Moreover, labour tax cuts offset by an increase in consumption taxes feed in part back into wages through indexation on consumer price inflation. This dampens the employment response to labour tax cuts through an increase in the reservation wage, as unemployment benefits are also indexed to inflation. Labour tax cuts offset by an increase in the corporate income tax have even a negative long-run output impact. This is because the multiplier effect of the ensuing drop in investment is much stronger than that of reduced social transfers – affecting mainly the disposable income of households – when tax cuts are matched by social security reform.

Table A1. **Main privatisations in Spain, 1986-99**

Society	Date	Per cent of capital sold	Receipts (Billions Pts)
Seat	1986	75.0	19
Telefónica	1987	..	82
Endesa	1988	20.0	74
Repsol	1989	26.4	135
Repsol	1989	4.2	21
Repsol	1990	2.9	19
Seat	1990	24.0	20
Repsol	1992	9.9	64
Repsol	1993	14.0	106
Argentaria	1993	24.9	69
Argentaria	1993	25.0	99
Endesa	1994	8.7	138
Repsol	1995	19.0	130
Telefónica	1995	12.0	165
Repsol	1996	11.0	140
Argentaria	1996	25.0	155
Gas Natural	1996	3.8	36
Telefónica	1997	20.9	630
Repsol	1997	10.0	169
Auxini	1997	60.0	6
Endesa	1997	25.0	660
Telefónica International (TISA)	1997	23.8	131
CSI (Aceralia)[1]	1997	60.0	222
Elcano	1997	100.0	6
Inespal	1997	100.0	62
Retevisión	1997	70.0	181
Aldeasa[2]	1997	100.0	56
Endesa	1998	41.1	1 490
Argentaria	1998	25.1	325
Tabacalera	1998	52.4	310
H.J. Barreras	1998	100.0	..
Enatcar	1999	..	26

1. Comprises four separate transactions: a sale of 35 per cent to the Luxembourg-based Arbed, and subsequently three sales to domestic firms.
2. Comprises two separate transactions: a sale of 30 per cent to the publicly controlled Tabacalera, and an IPO for 70 per cent.
Source: OECD Secretariat.

Table A2. **Main shareholdings in Latin American banks by BBV and BSCH**

1999

Country	Bank	Total assets [1]	Shareholdings (per cent)	Rank by asset
BBV				
Argentina	Banco Francés	1 256	60	3
Brazil	BBV Brasil	625	100	10
Colombia	Banco Ganadero	496	56	2
Chile	BHIF	419	44	7
Mexico	BBV México	1 213	67	6
Peru	Banco Continental	403	39	3
Puerto Rico	BBV Puerto Rico	506	100	3
Venezuela	Banco Provincial	799	51	1
BSCH				
Argentina	Banco Rio de la Plata	1 454	53	3
	Banco de Galicia	2 200	10	1
	Banco Tornquist	172	100	20
Bolivia	Banco Santa Cruz	223	90	1
Brazil	BS Brasil	836	89	14
	Banco de Noroeste	..	76	9
Colombia	BS Colombia	198	61	8
Chile	Banco Santiago	1 464	44	1
	BS Chile	1 278	89	2
Mexico	BS Mexicano	1 748	71	8
	Banco Bital	1 800	8	5
Paraguay	Banco Asunción	22	98	7
Peru	Bancosur	156	45	5
	BS Perú	276	100	4
Puerto Rico	BS Puerto Rico	1 255	79	2
Venezuela	Banco de Venezuela	367	98	3

1. In billions of pesetas.
Source: BBV and BSCH.

Annex III

Calendar of main economic events

1998

January

30-year government bond issue.

February

The Bank of Spain cuts its intervention rate by 25 basis points to 4.5 per cent.

Launch of the final stage of the privatisation of *Argentaria*.

Entry into force of the agreement on the out-of-court settlement of labour disputes, and of the interconfederal mediation and arbitration system (SIMA).

The central government and the trade unions conclude an agreement on the new Civil Service Charter, also signed with the regional governments. Wages to be set centrally and measures to improve the mobility of civil servants to be put in place.

March

The Council of Ministers approves, by Royal Decree, the extension of social cover to part-time workers.

Entry into force of the *Estatuto del Contribuyente*, which *inter alia* sets maximum time limits for tax refunds and inspections.

The Council of Ministers approves the new National Vocational Training Programme for the period 1998-2002.

April

Parliament approves the new law on land use which makes possible an increase in the supply of developable land by modifying the criteria of land classification and lowers from 15 per cent to a maximum of 10 per cent the portion of land that owners must cede to local authorities at the time of sale.

Scope of cuts in social security contributions (under the *Plan de Empleo*) widened to part-time permanent contracts, permanent contracts given to people who were self-employed, and contracts of people replacing women on maternity leave.

Launch of public offering for the government's stake in *Tabacalera*.

Parliament approves the draft law on the universal postal service.

May

The Bank of Spain cuts its intervention rate from 4.50 to 4.25 per cent.

The Council of Ministers approves a draft law on venture capital companies designed to make it easier for small and medium-sized companies to obtain capital. The main provisions of the law are greater flexibility in the management of venture capital company portfolios and the possibility for collective investment undertakings to manage and invest in venture capital companies.

Launch of public offering for the State's remaining stake in Endesa.

A third fixed-telephone licence is awarded to the Lince consortium (comprising France Telecom, Cableuropa and Editel).

July

Reduction in the price of domestic gas.

August

Entry into force of the decree taking certain drugs off the list of medicines reimbursed by the social security.

Entry into force of the new telecommunications charges of the dominant operator (increase in the price of local calls, reduction in the price of long distance calls, and billing of calls by the second).

September

Entry into force of the Hydrocarbons Law.

October

Parliament approves the Ley del Mercado de Valores, which brings Spanish regulations into line with European standards. Inter alia, this law provides for the free entry into the Spanish financial services market of firms from other EU countries on equal terms of competition.

The government adopts a decree restricting refunds of medicines to the price of the equivalent generic drug if it exists.

The Bank of Spain cuts its intervention rate from 4.25 to 3.75 per cent.

As part of the preparation of the 1999 budget, the government announces a reduction in withholding tax on the interest on bank accounts from 25 to 18 per cent as from 1 January 1999.

November

The government and the trade unions agree on a new part-time employment contract, with better social cover for the employees concerned.

The Bank of Spain lowers its intervention rate from 3.75 to 3.5 per cent.

December

The Bank of Spain cuts it intervention rate from 3.5 to 3.25 per cent.

The Comisión del Mercado de Telecomunicaciones awards new licences for fixed-telephone services.

The revenue guarantees for the regions are modified. In particular, the personal income tax revenue returned to the regions must grow at least in line with national gross domestic product.

The minimum wage for 1999 is increased by 1.8 per cent in line with inflation forecasts for 1999.

Parliament approves the 1999 budget and accompanying legislation. The target for the general government deficit is 1.6 per cent of GDP. The law also provides for the possibility of indemnifying electricity companies for the transition to a competitive regime, and of converting public hospitals into independently-run public health foundations.

The government announces its intention to partially privatise Iberia (with 30 per cent of the capital reserved to institutional investors).

1999

January

Entry into force of European Monetary Union.

Merger of the Banco Central Hispano and Banco de Santander.

Entry into force of the new part-time contract of employment with reduced employer contributions.

Entry into force of the personal income tax reform. The maximum marginal rate is cut from 56 to 48 per cent, and the minimum rate from 20 to 18 per cent.

March

Launch of a public offering for 66 per cent of the capital of Indra.

Launch of the privatisation of Enatcar.

Merger of three Galician savings banks.

The government sells off its remaining 30 per cent stake in Retevisión.

April

The European Central Bank lowers its intervention rate to 2.5 per cent.

The government adopts a package of emergency measures to stem the rise in consumer prices, by lowering certain controlled prices, particular those of electricity, natural gas, telecommunications, motorways and home purchase deeds. The package also includes measures to promote competition, in particular mandatory notification of company mergers to the Servicio de Defensa de la Competencia and acceleration of the timetable for the liberalisation of the gas sector.

The government announces the extension to the end of 1999 of the cuts in social security contributions for permanent new contracts given to certain categories of the population.

May

The Council of Ministers approves a preliminary draft Competition Law, the main provisions of which are: i) compulsory notification of planned mergers so that their impact on competition can be evaluated; ii) the competition watch-dog, Tribunal de Defensa de la Competencia, to verify that subsidies to public enterprises do not distort competition; iii) an increase in the Tribunal's resources.

The Council of Ministers approves a new Water Act, to be brought before Parliament.

June

Launch of the partial privatisation of Red Eléctrica.

Adoption of a new law on temporary employment agencies. The social rights and wages of temporary personnel have to be equivalent to those of other workers in the same firm doing a similar job.

July

The government announces a reduction in pharmaceutical wholesalers' margins (entry into force: 15 September 1999).

The government announces measures to combat inflation. The VAT rate on butane gas cylinders is cut from 16 to 7 per cent. Excise duties on petroleum products will be frozen in 2000. Competition in the fuel distribution sector to be stepped up.

October

The government presents a draft budget for 2000 which aims at a general government deficit of 0.8 per cent of GDP. The main measures include: an increase in minimum pensions, extension of unemployment coverage for the long-term unemployed with family responsibilities; an increase in tax expenditures – in respect of corporate income tax – for innovation and research and development.

The government extends the cuts in social security contributions for new indefinite-term contracts for the year 2000, while reducing those for people under 30 and increasing those for over 45-year-olds and the long-term unemployed. The reductions in contributions for the conversion of temporary contracts into permanent contracts are abolished.

The government announces a cut in the price of local telephone calls and authorises Telefónica to raise monthly subscriber charges from August 2000 (the increases should however still be less than the rise in consumer prices).

Merger of Argentaria and BBV.

November

The European Central Bank raises its intervention rate from 2.5 to 3 per cent.

Merger of two savings banks in the region of Navarra.

The central and regional governments approve the National Plan of Urban Waste, which foresees the implementation of measures for selective treatment of waste.

A decision of the Constitutional Court opens the way to regional competition regulators.

BASIC STATISTICS:

INTERNATIONAL COMPARISONS

	Units	Reference period [1]	Australia	Austria
Population				
Total	Thousands	1997	18 532	8 072
Inhabitants per sq. km	Number	1997	2	96
Net average annual increase over previous 10 years	%	1997	1.3	0.6
Employment				
Total civilian employment (TCE)[2]	Thousands	1997	8 430	3 685
of which:				
Agriculture	% of TCE	1997	5.2	6.8
Industry	% of TCE	1997	22.1	30.3
Services	% of TCE	1997	72.7	63.8
Gross domestic product (GDP)				
At current prices and current exchange rates	Bill. US$	1997	392.9	206.2
Per capita	US$	1997	21 202	25 549
At current prices using current PPPs[3]	Bill. US$	1997	406.8	186.3
Per capita	US$	1997	21 949	23 077
Average annual volume growth over previous 5 years	%	1997	4.1	1.9
Gross fixed capital formation (GFCF)	% of GDP	1997	21.5	24.1
of which:				
Machinery and equipment	% of GDP	1997	10.3 (96)	8.8 (96)
Residential construction	% of GDP	1997	4.4 (96)	6.2 (96)
Average annual volume growth over previous 5 years	%	1997	7.3	2.8
Gross saving ratio[4]	% of GDP	1997	18.4	23
General government				
Current expenditure on goods and services	% of GDP	1997	16.7	19.4
Current disbursements[5]	% of GDP	1996	34.8	48
Current receipts	% of GDP	1996	35.4	47.9
Net official development assistance	% of GNP	1996	0.28	0.24
Indicators of living standards				
Private consumption per capita using current PPP's[3]	US$	1997	13 585	12 951
Passenger cars, per 1 000 inhabitants	Number	1995	477	447
Telephones, per 1 000 inhabitants	Number	1995	510	465
Television sets, per 1 000 inhabitants	Number	1994	489	480
Doctors, per 1 000 inhabitants	Number	1996	2.5	2.8
Infant mortality per 1 000 live births	Number	1996	5.8	5.1
Wages and prices (average annual increase over previous 5 years)				
Wages (earnings or rates according to availability)	%	1998	1.5	5.2
Consumer prices	%	1998	2.0	1.8
Foreign trade				
Exports of goods, fob*	Mill. US$	1998	55 882	61 754
As % of GDP	%	1997	15.6	28.4
Average annual increase over previous 5 years	%	1998	5.6	9
Imports of goods, cif*	Mill. US$	1998	60 821	68 014
As % of GDP	%	1997	15.3	31.4
Average annual increase over previous 5 years	%	1998	7.5	7
Total official reserves[6]	Mill. SDR's	1998	10 942	14 628 (97)
As ratio of average monthly imports of goods	Ratio	1998	2.2	2.7 (97)

* At current prices and exchange rates.
1. Unless otherwise stated.
2. According to the definitions used in OECD Labour Force Statistics.
3. PPPs = Purchasing Power Parities.
4. Gross saving = Gross national disposable income minus private and government consumption.

EMPLOYMENT OPPORTUNITIES

Economics Department, OECD

The Economics Department of the OECD offers challenging and rewarding opportunities to economists interested in applied policy analysis in an international environment. The Department's concerns extend across the entire field of economic policy analysis, both macro-economic and microeconomic. Its main task is to provide, for discussion by committees of senior officials from Member countries, documents and papers dealing with current policy concerns. Within this programme of work, three major responsibilities are:

- to prepare regular surveys of the economies of individual Member countries;
- to issue full twice-yearly reviews of the economic situation and prospects of the OECD countries in the context of world economic trends;
- to analyse specific policy issues in a medium-term context for the OECD as a whole, and to a lesser extent for the non-OECD countries.

The documents prepared for these purposes, together with much of the Department's other economic work, appear in published form in the *OECD Economic Outlook, OECD Economic Surveys, OECD Economic Studies* and the Department's *Working Papers* series.

The Department maintains a world econometric model, INTERLINK, which plays an important role in the preparation of the policy analyses and twice-yearly projections. The availability of extensive cross-country data bases and good computer resources facilitates comparative empirical analysis, much of which is incorporated into the model.

The Department is made up of about 80 professional economists from a variety of backgrounds and Member countries. Most projects are carried out by small teams and last from four to eighteen months. Within the Department, ideas and points of view are widely discussed; there is a lively professional interchange, and all professional staff have the opportunity to contribute actively to the programme of work.

Skills the Economics Department is looking for:

a) Solid competence in using the tools of both microeconomic and macroeconomic theory to answer policy questions. Experience indicates that this normally requires the equivalent of a Ph.D. in economics or substantial relevant professional experience to compensate for a lower degree.

b) Solid knowledge of economic statistics and quantitative methods; this includes how to identify data, estimate structural relationships, apply basic techniques of time series analysis, and test hypotheses. It is essential to be able to interpret results sensibly in an economic policy context.

c) A keen interest in and extensive knowledge of policy issues, economic developments and their political/social contexts.

d) Interest and experience in analysing questions posed by policy-makers and presenting the results to them effectively and judiciously. Thus, work experience in government agencies or policy research institutions is an advantage.

e) The ability to write clearly, effectively, and to the point. The OECD is a bilingual organisation with French and English as the official languages. Candidates must have excellent knowledge of one of these languages, and some knowledge of the other. Knowledge of other languages might also be an advantage for certain posts.

f) For some posts, expertise in a particular area may be important, but a successful candidate is expected to be able to work on a broader range of topics relevant to the work of the Department. Thus, except in rare cases, the Department does not recruit narrow specialists.

g) The Department works on a tight time schedule with strict deadlines. Moreover, much of the work in the Department is carried out in small groups. Thus, the ability to work with other economists from a variety of cultural and professional backgrounds, to supervise junior staff, and to produce work on time is important.

General information

The salary for recruits depends on educational and professional background. Positions carry a basic salary from FF 318 660 or FF 393 192 for Administrators (economists) and from FF 456 924 for Principal Administrators (senior economists). This may be supplemented by expatriation and/or family allowances, depending on nationality, residence and family situation. Initial appointments are for a fixed term of two to three years.

Vacancies are open to candidates from OECD Member countries. The Organisation seeks to maintain an appropriate balance between female and male staff and among nationals from Member countries.

For further information on employment opportunities in the Economics Department, contact:

Management Support Unit
Economics Department
OECD
2, rue André-Pascal
75775 PARIS CEDEX 16
FRANCE

E-Mail: eco.contact@oecd.org

Applications citing ''ECSUR'', together with a detailed *curriculum vitae* in English or French, should be sent to the Head of Personnel at the above address.

The Electronic Advantage
Ask for our free Catalogue

The Fast and Easy way to work with statistics and graphs!

- Cut and paste capabilities
- Quick search & find functions
- Zoom for magnifying graphics
- Uses ACROBAT software
  (included free of charge)
- Works on Windows

OECD on the WEB: **www.oecd.org**

- ✂

Please **FAX** or **MAIL** this page to the OECD Paris,
—— or to one of the four OECD Centres (*see overleaf*) ——

○ I wish to receive the OECD Electronic Publications Catalogue **FREE OF CHARGE**

Name _____ Profession _____

Address _____

City _____ E-mail _____

Country _____

Area of interest _____

Where to send your request:

In Austria, Germany and Switzerland

OECD Centre Bonn
August-Bebel-Allee 6,
D-53175 Bonn
Tel.: (49-228) 959 1215
Fax: (49-228) 959 1218
E-mail: bonn.contact@oecd.org
Internet: www.oecd.org/bonn

In Latin America

OECD Centre Mexico
Edificio INFOTEC
Av. San Fernando No. 37
Col. Toriello Guerra
Tlalpan C.P. 14050,
Mexico D.F.
Tel.: (52-5) 528 10 38
Fax: (52-5) 606 13 07
E-mail: mexico.contact@oecd.org
Internet: rtn.net.mx/ocde/

In the United States

OECD Center Washington
2001 L Street N.W., Suite 650
Washington, DC 20036-4922
Tel.: (202) 785 6323
Toll free: (1 800) 456-6323
Fax: (202) 785 0350
E-mail: washington.contact@oecd.org
Internet: www.oecdwash.org

In Asia

OECD Centre Tokyo
Landic Akasaka Bldg.
2-3-4 Akasaka, Minato-ku,
Tokyo 107-0052
Tel.: (81-3) 3586 2016
Fax: (81-3) 3584 7929
E-mail : center@oecdtokyo.org
Internet: www.oecdtokyo.org

In the rest of the world

OECD Paris Centre
2 rue André-Pascal, 75775 Paris Cedex 16, France
Fax: 33 (0)1 49 10 42 76 **Tel:** 33 (0)1 49 10 42 35
E-mail : sales@oecd.org
Internet : www.oecd.org
Online Orders: www.oecd.org/publications *(secure payment with credit card)*

OECD PUBLICATIONS, 2, rue André-Pascal, 75775 PARIS CEDEX 16
PRINTED IN FRANCE
(10 2000 24 1 P) ISBN 92-64-17524-5 – No. 51085 2000
ISSN 0376-6438